PSYCHOLOGY RESEARCH PROGRESS

IMPRISONMENT AND INCARCERATION

PATTERNS, PROSPECTS AND PSYCHOLOGICAL IMPLICATIONS

PSYCHOLOGY RESEARCH PROGRESS

Additional books in this series can be found on Nova's website under the Series tab.

Additional e-books in this series can be found on Nova's website under the e-book tab.

PSYCHOLOGY RESEARCH PROGRESS

IMPRISONMENT AND INCARCERATION

PATTERNS, PROSPECTS AND PSYCHOLOGICAL IMPLICATIONS

HILLARY N. CLARKSON
EDITOR

nova publishers
New York

Library of Congress Cataloging-in-Publication Data

Imprisonment and incarceration : patterns, prospects and psychological implications / editor: Hillary N. Clarkson.
pages cm. -- (Psychology research progress)
Includes index.
ISBN 978-1-63482-117-9 (hardcover)
1. Imprisonment. 2. Prisons. I. Clarkson, Hillary N.
HV8705.I473 2015
365--dc23
2015002248

Published by Nova Science Publishers, Inc. † New York

Contents

PREFACE

Aside from capital punishment, incarceration represents the most severe and most costly punishment that state governments can administer to its citizens. The use of incarceration has garnered increasing attention over the years, particularly in the United States where incarcerated populations have undergone approximately forty years of nearly continuous growth. In examining the differences in prisonization and survival strategies between the sexes, research has found that male inmates often enlist gang members for protection, while women recreate family for emotional support. This book examines the conventional identities of both sexes behind the walls of imprisonment, and global trends in incarceration. The book also contributes to the discussion on the education of women in situations of deprivation of liberty and provides an in-depth investigation of reform through interpreting how a selected group of men who have desisted from heroin-use understand and present their change process. Finally, this book discusses the psychological implications of being incarcerated and the patterns and prospects of imprisonment.

Chapter 1 – Inmates assume different roles during the course of incarceration to survive the pains of imprisonment. It is believed that women feel the pains of imprisonment more harshly than males because of the difficulty in being separated from their family and children. Adaptations to the prison environment differ according to sex, yet, both sexes can succumb to prisonization. Prisonization impacts disciplinary infractions and rates of recidivism. Although women are not more violent than men in prison, they tend to be cited more for rule violating behavior. Since an inmate's associates in prison impacts institutional behavior, being associated with a supportive pseudo family can prevent periods of maladjustment, in addition to serving as a strong source of support for rehabilitative and reintegrative success.

Involvement in prosocial prison activities, with associates committed to supporting newfound conventional identities, can modify rule breaking conduct and assist in the reinforcement of conventional behavior. Prison-based educational/vocational programs are correlated with reduced disciplinary infractions and recidivism, but the impact of less traditional prison-based programs is lacking. Furthermore, research shows that the traditional pseudo family is weakening, demonstrating the need for women to rely on other alternatives to serve as networks of support. To shed light on this neglected area in the literature, the author conducted a study that analyzed rates of disciplinary infractions and recidivism among female prisoners that worked in two HIV prison-based peer programs (ACE & CARE). Results showed that working in programs like ACE/CARE prevented periods of maladjustment and subsequent disciplinary infractions during incarceration. Such programs served as an extended family unit for female inmates and minimized their pains of imprisonment. Family was recreated in a supportive environment that provided encouragement for the establishment of newfound conventional identities. These relationships continued outside of the prison walls, provided women with familial support upon release, and subsequently resulted in increased levels of postrelease success for female offenders.

Chapter 2 – Since its initial publication in 1999, the World Prison Population List has documented an approximately 25% increase in the global prison population from more than 8 million incarcerated persons to more than 10.2 million as of October 2013. While substantial in absolute terms, this growth in incarceration may not be universal as three nations (United States, China, and Russia) have accounted for nearly half of the world's incarcerated population during this time. Due to this disproportionate representation, any changes in the incarcerated populations in these three nations would predominate changes in other nations. Indeed, incarceration growth over time is neither inevitable nor universal as evidenced by nations such as Finland which experienced a substantial decrease in the use of incarceration since the early 1950s. Using data from the International Centre for Prison Studies, this chapter explores global trends in incarceration and assesses the extent to which growth in incarceration was experienced throughout the world since the early 1990s. Special attention is given to trends in the composition of incarcerated populations in regards to remand and female prisoners. Several suggestions are made for future research on cross-national differences in incarceration use.

Chapter 3 – This paper forms part of the discussion on education in prisons, which has received attention in the field of human rights. The right to education in the context of deprivation of liberty is on the agenda of international discussions, and is aligned to the concerns about the situation of women prisoners. The empirical material was collected in a research that analyzed the constitution of all school educational experiences of women, young and adults, in situations of imprisonment in 04 Brazilian exclusively female prisons. The discussions presented in the article refer specifically to reports produced on interviews with 11 women who attend school in one of these institutions. The analysis of the narratives produced by the interviewees takes as reference the theory of the relationship with knowledge proposed by Bernard Charlot, in a specific manner, the concepts of mobilization, direction and activity. The reports of the school experiences show two different situations regarding the conditions of access and permanence in basic education: trajectories marked by difficulties, stopped early, others more regular and long lasting. The prison is therefore for some women, the possibility of resuming the elementary school, for others, the inability to pursue high school. Despite these differences, it is possible to identify the aspects common to the reports, regarding the senses of school education, the mobilization in relation to learning and the positive effects of schooling. These aspects are presented and discussed as elements of understanding the complex reality of the education of women in the prison system.

Chapter 4 – This study presents an in-depth investigation of reform through interpreting how a selected group of men who have desisted from heroin-use understand and present their change process. It consisted of ten life narratives including the stories of seven successful desisters and three active offenders living in Hong Kong. The 'opportunity' sample was recruited with the assistance of one non-governmental organization which provides help with discharged prisoners. Based upon the interview data, a thematic content analysis revealed that successful desistance was dependent upon two contingencies, namely deterioration of physical health and religious conviction. In addition, an actor's display of agency through readiness and openness to change was the precursor for establishing an identity shift incompatible with continued criminal behavior. Belief in the good core self encouraged ex-prisoners to achieve 'earned redemption' through engaging in generative pursuits. Desistance from drug-use behavior can be explained with reference to the interplay between individual decision and life-changes.

In: Imprisonment and Incarceration
Editor: Hillary N. Clarkson

ISBN: 978-1-63482-117-9

Chapter 1

CULTIVATING A PRISON COMMUNITY: ESTABLISHING CONVENTIONAL IDENTITIES BEHIND THE WALLS AND BEYOND

Kimberly Collica-Cox*[*]*, PhD
PACE University, US

ABSTRACT

Inmates assume different roles during the course of incarceration to survive the pains of imprisonment. It is believed that women feel the pains of imprisonment more harshly than males because of the difficulty in being separated from their family and children. Adaptations to the prison environment differ according to sex, yet, both sexes can succumb to prisonization. Prisonization impacts disciplinary infractions and rates of recidivism. Although women are not more violent than men in prison, they tend to be cited more for rule violating behavior. Since an inmate's associates in prison impacts institutional behavior, being associated with a supportive pseudo family can prevent periods of maladjustment, in addition to serving as a strong source of support for rehabilitative and reintegrative success. Involvement in prosocial prison activities, with associates committed to supporting newfound conventional identities, can

[*]Contact Information: Dr. Kimberly Collica-Cox; Associate Professor; PACE University; Criminal Justice & Security; Dyson College of Arts and Sciences; 41 Park Row; 11th Floor/Room 1126; New York, NY 10038; (212) 346-1862; 212-346-1435 (Fax); kcollicacox@pace.edu.

modify rule breaking conduct and assist in the reinforcement of conventional behavior. Prison-based educational/vocational programs are correlated with reduced disciplinary infractions and recidivism, but the impact of less traditional prison-based programs is lacking. Furthermore, research shows that the traditional pseudo family is weakening, demonstrating the need for women to rely on other alternatives to serve as networks of support. To shed light on this neglected area in the literature, the author conducted a study that analyzed rates of disciplinary infractions and recidivism among female prisoners that worked in two HIV prison-based peer programs (ACE & CARE). Results showed that working in programs like ACE/CARE prevented periods of maladjustment and subsequent disciplinary infractions during incarceration. Such programs served as an extended family unit for female inmates and minimized their pains of imprisonment. Family was recreated in a supportive environment that provided encouragement for the establishment of newfound conventional identities. These relationships continued outside of the prison walls, provided women with familial support upon release, and subsequently resulted in increased levels of postrelease success for female offenders.

THE PAINS OF PRISONIZATION FOR WOMEN

Both sexes adapt differently to incarceration, yet, the process of prisonization occurs for both male and female prisoners. Inmates become ensconced within the inmate subculture and invested in the inmate code (i.e., snitches gets stitches, stay out of the business of others, keep calm and cool, etc) (Sykes & Messinger, 1960), a code in conflict with conventional norms (Clemmer, 1940). The longer the period of incarceration, the more likely an inmate will become prisonized (Clemmer, 1940). In examining the differences in prisonization and survival strategies between the sexes, research finds that male inmates often enlist as gang members for protection, while women recreate family for emotional support (Pollack-Byrne, 1990). When compared to males, females are much less likely to have relationships based on intimidation and they are more likely to form supportive social networks (Jiang & Winfree, 2006). The dynamics of the prison experience are very different for men and women.

Giallombardo (1966) conducted one of the earliest studies of the female inmate subculture and concluded that the recreation of family is used as a coping mechanism. Since Giallombardo's study, there are mixed results in the literature regarding fictive families. Same sex coupling may be overestimated and in cases of its existence, the relationship tends to fulfill more emotional than sexual needs (Cranford & Williams, 1998; Jones, 1993; Propper, 1982). These prison-based families are usually identified as play families, pseudo families, make believe families, or fictive families (Collica, 2010).

> They can resemble the traditional nuclear family unit (i.e., jail-mom, jail-dad, and jail-children), the single-parent household (i.e., jail-mom and jail-children) or incorporate extended family members (i.e., jail-siblings, jail-aunts, jail-uncles, etc). Pseudo families can include the development of consensual same sex relationships, in which one inmate will portray the father figure, typically known as the "butch" or "aggressor," and another will play the mother figure, known as the "femme." Both inmates can assist their jail-children in adapting to the inmate subculture. They may prevent them from engaging in troublesome behaviors, while also teaching them how to navigate the prison environment (Collica, 2010, p. 318-319).

We do not find evidence of these families in correctional institutions outside of the U.S., making the creation of the fictive family unique to American prison culture (Humphrey, 1987). Other studies denote a decrease in fictive families associated with an increase in vocational and educational programming availability (Fox, 1984).

Women recreate family to manage the pain associated with the separation from their family, particularly their children. The Bureau of Justice Statistics finds that an estimated 1.7 million children in the U.S. have an incarcerated parent (Glaze & Maruschak, 2010). One-quarter of incarcerated parents have a child under the age of four and one-third of minors will reach the age of 18 before their parent(s) are released from prison (Glaze & Maruschak, 2010). Seventy percent of incarcerated women have a minor child. While incarcerated, a female prisoner's children are usually cared for by another female member of her family (most frequently the grandparents), whereas when men are incarcerated, it is typically the mother who will raise the children (Glaze & Maruschak, 2010; Snell & Morton, 1994). Prison makes it especially difficult for female inmates to maintain family contact since many states only have one female facility; female inmates have no hope of transferring to another facility that might bring them closer to where their family resides (Genders & Player, 1990). Most facilities are in rural areas, whereas most family resides in urban areas. Family contact is very limited because of the distance and the costs associated with travel (Mackenzie, Robinson and Campbell 1989; Reed & Reed, 2004). Therefore, women receive fewer visits from their children. When women are in prison, children are often relocated (Greenfield & Snell, 2000). If visits are possible, they are closely monitored. Other forms of communication, such as phone calls and mail are also closely monitored, further increasing the pains of separation (Genders & Player, 1990). Throughout the course of their incarceration, women worry about their children and they worry about being able to maintain meaningful bonds (Belknap, 2001).

PRISON ACCLIMATION & PRISON-BASED PROGRAMMING

How offenders acclimate to incarceration can severely impact their rate of disciplinary infractions, in addition to their ability to successfully transition back into the community upon release. Stress can lead to poor adjustment and consequently, poor behavior. If maladaptive behavior persists, it is likely to encumber rehabilitative efforts (Clemmer, 1940; Irwin & Cressey, 1962). For the rehabilitative process to be successful, offenders need to create conventional networks of support to encourage prosocial behavior (Sommers, Baskin & Fagan, 1994). Prosocial networks are critical in the rehabilitative process (Reisig, Holtfreter, & Morash, 2002) and these networks can be created behind bars (Collica, 2010). There is evidence that female relationships in prison can be supportive (Severance, 2005). Nevertheless, female inmates report a great amount of distrust between one another (Greer, 2000; Severance, 2005) and if fictive families are in decline (Fox, 1984), it becomes extremely important to establish new sources of support for female offenders.

Offenders can find necessary support from involvement in prison programs and supportive networks that develop from being a participant in such programs. Prison programs can provide offenders with conventional support during incarceration, and after incarceration when offenders may feel the most isolated and alone (Koons, Burrow, Morash & Bynum, 1997; Severance 2005).

Female offenders are in greater need for programming when compared to their male counterparts. According to Lahman (2000), female inmates have fewer academic and vocational opportunities available to them in prison than their male counterparts (Miller, 1990). The greatest disparity in prison programming between male and female inmates is for vocational opportunity. Prison-based vocational programming not only have the opportunity to provide offenders with marketable job skills but to further aid in the rehabilitative process by cultivating prosocial networks. A decision to maintain a deficient level of vocational programming is a wasted opportunity.

Since most states only have one female correctional facility (whereas men are sent to different facilities based on their needs and the programming offered), many programs in women's facilities are gender-based. These programs prepare women to work in traditional pink-collar employment (i.e., secretarial, sewing, food service, etc.), which results in the attainment of low wage employment upon release (Lahman, 2000). Conversely, men are trained in traditional blue-collar jobs (air conditioning repair, plumbing, electronics, etc.), which permits them to obtain better employment opportunities upon release. When women lack vital skills for today's workforce, they are unable to support their family after release. Females are still being trained for "unstable" and "underpaid" jobs (Lahman, 2000). The subservient role of women in society is reflected within the prison environment, as prison is often a larger reflection of societal problems like racism, classism, and sexism. Gender-based acquiescent roles are perpetuated by the correctional system in its failure to provide skills-equality (Moyer, 1984; Smart, 1976; Zaitzow & Thomas, 2003). Due to their smaller numbers, prison administrators are able to justify evading the programmatic needs of female inmates (Bonta, Pang, & Wallace-Capretta, 1995).

If employed while incarcerated, most female prisoners are assigned to domestic work, which does not teach women relevant job skills and offers little in terms of emotional support (Shover, 1991); its only purpose is to aid in the daily maintenance of the institution (Dobash Dobash, & Gutteridge, 1986; Pollack-Byrne, 1990). There is little to no opportunity for rehabilitation, for the attainment of valuable job skills, or for the creation of prosocial networks, all of which would promote conventional behavior upon release (Pollack-Byrne, 1990). "Decisions about what to teach [women in the prison environment] have been decided largely on the basis of institutional needs as well as notions about what is appropriate work for women" (Moyer, 1984, p. 54).

Female pathways to incarceration are often paved by long roads of sexual and physical abuse, substance abuse histories, and limited employment skills. Prisons have the opportunity, through programming, to address these needs and to encourage the prosocial bonds necessary for rehabilitative outcomes. Support groups, inmate peers, and civilian staff in faith-based programming serve as supportive networks and are essential factors for successful reintegration (Parsons & Warner-Robbins, 2002). Effective prison-based programming will offer women emotional support in an environment that allows them to comfortably share their feelings (Koons, Burrow, Morash, & Bynum, 1997). "Over time, the women became close, began to turn to one another for support, and formed sister-like relationships. Program staff members viewed this as part of the healing process (Koons et al. 1997, p. 525)."

Disciplinary Behavior and Prison-Based Programming

Overall, prison-based educational programs dominate an inmate's time, constrain destructive influences (Harer, 1995) and reduce disciplinary infractions (Taylor, 1993). Programs can give inmates a reason to abide by prison rules (Taylor, 1992), particularly if a poor disciplinary record might led to program removal. Studies demonstrate a link between prison programs and reduced disciplinary infractions, increased employment upon release and diminished recidivism rates (Gerber & Fritsch, 1995). Some prison programs will prove to be more successful than others based on a multitude of factors, such as remaining separate from the rest of facility to minimize distractions, affording a substitute community, imparting marketable job skills, offering post release services, and hiring dedicated staff who can form supportive relationships with offenders (Collica, 2002; Gerber & Fritsch, 1995; Koons et al. 1997; Linden & Perry, 1982;). Cultivating conventional conduct and relationships are attainable goals of prison-based programs; program staff is integral to this process irrespective of program focus (Collica-Cox, 2014).

Program effectiveness will also vary based on individual characteristics; not all programs will work for all offenders and female offenders, whose pathways to incarceration differ from their male counterparts, may find more success with programs that are gendered-focused (Collica-Cox, 2014; Gover, Perez, & Jennings, 2008). Women prisoners are less violent than men but they are cited for disciplinary infractions more often. In the last report compiled by the Bureau of Justice Statistics (BJS) (Stephan, 1989), inmates averaged 1.5 infractions annually. It is difficult to know the "real" rate of infractions since the decision on whether or not to write the infraction is based upon the correctional officer's discretion; inmates commit more infractions than reported (Casey-Acevedo & Bakken, 2003; Hewitt, Poole & Regoli, 1984). Women are two times more likely to be written-up for minor infractions than their male counterparts (Eaton, 1993). Men acquire 1.4 infractions per year, while women obtain two infractions per year (Stephan, 1989). There is an "assumption that women are irrational, compulsive and slightly neurotic" (Smart, 1976), in addition to being "too emotional," "too manipulative," and "too vocal" (Debell, 2001, p. 59). Even though women commit less serious infractions than men, they are punished more severely (Cao, Zhao, & Van Dine, 1997; Craddock, 1996; Kruttschnitt & Krmpotich, 1990; Lindquist, 1980; Stephan, 1989); the same behavior, when committed by men, is often overlooked (Casey-Acevedo & Bakken, 2003; Dalley, 1993; Dobash, Dobash & Gutteridge, 1986; Jiang, 2005; McClellan, 1994).

Women are more expressive than men, particularly regarding feelings of anger (Cranford & Williams, 1998; Suter, Bryne, Bryne, Howells & Day, 2002). Most of their expressions are non-violent but can be viewed by staff as constituting a disciplinary infraction, such as insubordination, creating a disturbance, verbal harassment of an officer, or even inciting a riot. Since men and women express themselves differently, what may actually be a healthy way of releasing pent up emotions may be perceived as problematic behavior (i.e., emotional outburst) for the female inmate. "When staff expect women to be more troublesome than men, and expand more energy in the detection and punishment of their misbehaviors, it is little wonder that women have high disciplinary rates" (Humphrey, 1987, p. 5). Overall, women are more likely than men to be cited for non-violent sexual offenses, while men are more likely to be cited for fighting offenses (Craddock, 1996). Both male and female prisoners are cited most often for disobeying a direct order (Tischler & Marquart, 1989). Some facilities may have a small group of chronic women offenders cited for violent behavior but it is atypical of female offenders as a whole (Casey-Acevedo & Bakken, 2003).

Participation in prison-based programming is one way to alleviate maladaptive behaviors and subsequently decrease disciplinary infractions. It provides a distraction from the dull routine of prison life, lessens frustrations (Tootoonchi, 1993) and occupies the inmates' time with a conventional approach (Taylor, 1992). Establishing conventional relationships with class participants and program staff help to promote conventional behavior (Collica, 2010). Inmate participants are positive role models for other inmates, which aids in bolstering their self-esteem (Taylor, 1993; Taylor, 1992). Self-esteem is not just an important factor in maintaining a law-abiding lifestyle, it is vital for female offenders, often plagued with poor self-image (Tewksbury & Vito, 1994).

Prison Programming and Recidivism

Research indicates that prison-based educational programs can promote reintegrative and rehabilitative outcomes, most notable are the reduced recidivism rates (Correctional Educational Bulletin, 2002; McCollum, 1994; Shrum, 2004), particularly when we examine the relationship between reduced recidivism and a college education (Gerber & Fritsch, 1995). Prison programming can provide offenders a real chance at leading conventional lifestyles and achieving the American Dream (Taylor, 1992).

Prison-based programming can provide offenders with new skills and/or enhance skills they possessed prior to incarceration (Tootoonchi, 1993). Participants in prison-based college programs are more likely to obtain stable employment upon release when compared to inmates who did not participate in a college program (Taylor, 1993). Numerous studies show a correlation between inmates with a GED and higher rates of employment, lower rates of unemployment, and lower rates of repeated criminal behavior when compared to those inmates without a GED (Gerber & Fitsch, 1995; Nuttall et al. 2002). "Most empirical research indicates that pre-college education leads to more favorable patterns of employment and postrelease education among participants" (Gerber & Fitsch, 1995, p. 127).

Education is not the only pathway to rehabilitative success. Post-release success can also be achieved through prison-based vocational programming:

> "The lack of a vocational skill is a major barrier to the reintegration of the prisoner into the community. It has also been shown that if an offender possesses a marketable job skill, employer objection to his criminal record is reduced significantly" (Enocksson, 1980, p. 11).

Vocational programs can offer inmates relevant job skills. Most jobs held within the prison system (i.e., porter) provide few work-related skills and have little utility in the outside job market (Schumacker, Anderson & Anderson, 1990). In absence of an effective vocational program, correctional facilities "run the risk of creating workers whose skills are suited only to an institutional setting" (Koski, 1998, p. 158). Participation in a vocational program is correlated with reduced recidivism (Canestrini, 1993; MacDonald, 1995). Inmates who participated in both educational and vocational programming had the highest rates of employment and the lowest rates of recidivism, when compared to groups who did not participate in any programming and to those groups that only participated in academic programming. Vocational completers showed higher employment rates and lower recidivism rates than non-vocational completers but academic only completers had the lowest rates of employment and the second highest levels of recidivism (Schumacker et al. 1990).

What About Non-Traditional Prison-Based Programming?

Research demonstrates that educational and vocational prison-based programs direct successful reentry outcomes, but it is unknown if we can generalize these findings to all prison programs. Little research has been conducted on less traditional vocational opportunities behind bars, such as HIV/AIDS peer education programs. HIV prison-based peer programs are not given the attention they deserve in the literature, especially as it relates to female inmates. Working in an HIV peer education program can help inmates to acquire essential employment skills that lead to an increased adherence to conventionality, resulting in reduced recidivism and prison disciplinary infractions.

The current exploratory study investigates two HIV prison-based peer education programs, ACE (AIDS, Counseling and Education) and CARE (Counseling, Aids, Resource and Education), which allowed female offenders to form conventional relationships within a different type of *play family*. This research examined if HIV peer programs could affect the process of criminal desistance and behavior modification for female inmates by influencing prison adjustment, prison disciplinary infractions, and post-release adjustment. The development of this prosocial network subsequently prevented prisonization by allowing female offenders to cultivate strong conventional attachments and strong networks of support, thereby increasing rates of institutional and postrelease success. Overall, participation as a HIV peer educator mitigated disciplinary infractions and reduced recidivism rates.

Methodology

This study, based on the narratives of 49 female offenders, examined the effects of two HIV prison-based peer programs on inmate peers in NYS (New York State): The ACE (AIDS, Counseling and Education) Program located at

Bedford Hills Correctional Facility (BHCF) and the CARE (Counseling, AIDS, Resource and Education) Program located at Taconic Correctional Facility (TCF). BHCF is the only maximum-security prison for women in NYS, holding approximately 800 inmates, and TCF, located across the street from BHCF, is a medium-security facility for women in NYS, holding approximately 400 inmates (at the time of the interviews). Since TCF is a medium-security facility, many women at BHCF who worked for ACE will work for CARE if drafted to TCF. ACE/CARE civilians work in both facilities. Both programs, in existence since the late 1980s, were created to deal with the AIDS epidemic in female prisons and provide a variety of services to inmate population such as support groups, education, crisis counseling, HIV testing, discharge planning, special events, professional trainings, etc. ACE educates over 3,000 women annually and CARE educates approximately 600 women annually. The programs consist of five civilians when fully staffed: a CARE Coordinator, an ACE Coordinator, a HIV Test Counselor, a HIV Discharge Planner, and an Upstate Supervisor. The number of inmate peers vary (anywhere from 4 to 9 for each program). Inmates in this sample worked for ACE/CARE for an average of 4 years, ranging from 6 months to 13 years and most were not HIV positive (86% and 14% respectively). Inmates were trained to provide counseling, educational workshops, and facilitate support groups. In addition, they had permission to work with specialized prison groups such as the nursery mothers, those in the behavioral health unit, those in hospice care, etc.

Prospective peer workers must have or be working toward their GED. All are required to submit a resume, to have successfully completed the HIV professional training series (offered by CARE/ACE), undergo two interviews (one by the program coordinator and one by the other inmate peers), and teach a demonstration lesson. Prospective workers must have a good disciplinary record during the months directly preceding employment. Inmates with poor records are encouraged to maintain good behavior for a few months before reapplying. A poor disciplinary record, once hired, is grounds for dismissal. Upon securing a peer position, each inmate staff member is supervised by a civilian (either the ACE or CARE Coordinator) from a community-based organization. Together, the civilians and inmates not only deliver comprehensive HIV related services, they create a supportive, community-oriented environment within the prison.

Sample

The sample for this study included: (a) women incarcerated in BHCF and TCF who were currently working as peer educators for ACE or CARE, (b) women incarcerated in one of NYS' five female facilities (Albion, Bayview, Beacon, Bedford Hills, or Taconic) who had previously worked as peer educators for ACE/CARE or both programs, and (c) formerly incarcerated women living in the community who, during their incarceration, had worked for ACE, CARE, or both programs. The author collected data from the peers over a seven month period, yielding a sample of 49 women. All participation was voluntary (no incentives were allowed) and all interviews were conducted in private. Forty-nine percent of the women were formerly incarcerated (n=24) and 51% of the women were currently incarcerated (n=25). [1]Based upon extensive one-on-one semi-structured interviews with these women, the author utilized a snowball/chain referral sample to obtain additional subjects. Out of 57 women that were identified and located by the author as matching the study's eligibility requirements (i.e., a current/former peer worker for ACE/CARE), seven women declined to participate, and one woman, incarcerated at Albion, was unable to be interviewed, yielding a response rate of 86%. Many questions required open-ended responses and yielded in-depth answers that could not easily be reduced to numerical format. The author examined common themes in answers generated by respondents according to the Grounded Theory Approach (Glasser & Strauss, 1967). Responses were recorded in written format by the author (tape recording was prohibited) and transcribed later that day. Categorization of responses and themes continued during transcription. It was believed that the use of both quantitative and qualitative measures would increase the validity of subjects' responses and provide a fuller understanding of their experiences.

The data on disciplinary infractions was collected as part of a larger research project on HIV peer programs; the survey for peer participants in the larger study was a revised version of Hirschi's questionnaire in his book, *Causes of Delinquency* (1969), to measure the strength of bonds between the female peers, the peers and the civilians, and the peers in relation to their

[1]The author worked with the creators of ACE/CARE to devise a list of all women who worked for both programs. Out of approximately 65 women identified, 49 were interviewed. Women not included were deported, deceased or unable to be located. Hence, 75% of all women who worked for both programs participated in this study. Snowball sampling, though not ideal, was the only way to locate subjects. The DOCCS (Department of Corrections and Community Supervision) does not keep records on peer workers.

overall commitment to the ACE/CARE Program. Many of Hirschi's questions were modified by the author and are now applicable to prisoners. Questions were borrowed from Sampson and Laub's study (1990) on Life Course Theory, which expanded upon Hirschi's original concept, to measure the strength of job stability, commitment, etc. Others were revised questions from research conducted by Alarid, Burton & Cullen (2000), Canter (1982), Friedman and Rosenbaum (1988), Lasley (1998), Rankin (1976), Shover et al. (1979), and Rosenbaum (1987). The author devised additional questions to measure social bonding, as well as questions that tapped into specific demographic information and specific information about the women's experiences working in ACE/CARE.

In this study, institutional success was measured in terms of disciplinary infractions and the number of tickets an inmate received during the course of her incarceration. To determine if working in ACE/CARE had an effect on the rate of tickets incurred, respondents were asked to report on the total number of tickets they received prior to and during the time they were employed with ACE/CARE. Inmates were asked how they would describe their own disciplinary history, if they perceived themselves as a disciplinary problem and if they felt that others perceived them as a disciplinary problem. Inmates in NYS receive "tickets" for misbehavior, such as Tier I (the least serious), Tier II or Tier III (the most serious). Punishments can include loss of packages, visits, program(s), employment, educational programming, commissary, phone calls, or fines and/or segregation.

Degrees of disciplinary infractions were measured by asking respondents how many disciplinary tickets they received, the severity of the disciplinary, and if the disciplinary infraction resulted in "keep-lock" status (being confined to their cell 23 out of 24 hours a day) or SHU (Special Housing Unit) status (being confined to segregative housing 23 out of 24 hours per day). Levels of institutional success were tested by comparing the number of disciplinary infractions each woman received before, during, and if applicable, after employment with the ACE/CARE program. It was hypothesized that a high percentage of women who worked in ACE/CARE (independent variable) would report a low number of disciplinary infractions while working for the program(s) (dependent variable). For those women living in the community, rates of recidivism (either re-arrest or a parole violation) were compared to the rates of recidivism for all women living in New York State. An additional measure of success was accessed by current job stability (i.e., if they were employed, how long they had been in their current position, if their work was regarded highly by their employer, etc.).

Demographics of the sample differed slightly from the average NYS female prisoner. In this sample, whites tended to be overrepresented (33% compared to a 22% rate among the study population), and the age of participants tended to be four years older (40 years old compared to an average of 36 years old among the study population) than the average NYS female inmate. All women had the equivalent to a high school education or higher and 43% of the sample was unemployed prior to their incarceration.

In terms of family status, 59% (n=29) stated that they had children, while 41% (n=20) reported not having any children. For those that had children (n=29), 41% (n=12) had one child, 38% (n=11) had two children, 7% (n=2) had three children, 7% (n=2) had four children, 3% (n=1) had 5 children, and 3% (n=1) had 7 children. Moreover, four of these women (14%) reported having one child that was deceased. The children of these women ranged in age from the youngest being two weeks old, while the oldest was 39 years old. Out of these 58 children, 36% were 18 years old or younger. Over one-half (61%) of sample participants were unmarried.

Many of the subjects (33%) were charged with multiple crimes. In terms of their most serious charge, 49% (n=24) were serving time for murder or manslaughter, 31% (n=15) were serving time for a drug-related offense, 12% (n=6) were serving time for assault, and 2% were serving time for robbery (n=1), burglary (n=1), kidnapping (n=1), or forgery (n=1). For subjects that were incarcerated (n=25), the average time served at the time of the interview was 11 years and six months. For subjects that were residing in the community (n=24), the average time served in prison was eight years and eight months. On average, interviews took approximately one hour and fifteen minutes to complete; the shortest interview lasted 35 minutes, while the longest interview lasted 140 minutes. All participation was voluntary (no incentives were allowed) and all interviews were conducted in private. Private rooms were set aside for prison interviews and interviews with formerly incarcerated subjects were conducted in their homes, offices, or another place of their choosing.

FINDINGS

To investigate the pains of imprisonment for women prisoners, participants were asked questions regarding stressful experiences behind bars. Over half (53%) cited separation from family as the most difficult part of being incarcerated, particularly the constant worry about their children and how they were being treated:

> "[The most stressful part was] not being with my children and worrying about where they were and what they were doing. My three younger sons ended up in foster care and for the first three years they were with a really nice woman who took really great care of them. I always knew she was using those checks for my kids because they always looked nice when they came to see me. But then her man cheated on her and she left him and couldn't keep my kids. They ended up with these horrible people, because they hardly do a background check and most of these people are in it for the check, and she never spent any of that money on my kids. Now that I have them back, I know something must have happened to them but they don't talk about it. My youngest one eats away all of his depression. He told me that when he used to visit me, he would pray for the gates to get stuck so that he could stay with me." (Blondie/CARE)

Other women struggled with the death of a family member while incarcerated or attempting to accept the loss of their youth. Women were also distressed over inconsistent rule enforcement, the dehumanization process of incarceration, parole board appearances, possessing limited freedom and privacy, and an overwhelming feeling of powerlessness:

> The most stressful part is having no control over your life. When they say jump, you jump. (Kate/ACE)

> "[The most stressful part was] having to deal with COs yelling at you, belittling you, and you can't say anything. You could write them up but nothing happens to them." (Scarlet/ACE)

For the time that the women worked in the program(s), they felt that the ACE/CARE peers and civilian staff served as a source of support during stressful times. Eighty-six percent of participants had at least one peer in ACE/CARE they considered to be their best friend. When asked if they found their inmate coworkers to be helpful during stressful times, 98% found support among their peers:

> "We had a bond. We were like a body. One person was the head, one a leg, and one a foot. We came together like a body, like a family. There was a spiritual bonding between us of love and caring and working toward the same goal." (Compassionate/ACE)

> "They were also part of our family. It was such a good cause and everyone was so sure of it and believed in it. We were determined and never gave up." (Freedom/ACE)

When asked if they found the ACE/CARE civilian staff to be supportive during such periods, 94% agreed:

> "They have always been supportive. Their goal was the same goal as ours. They believed in the education and care for the patients." (Compassionate/ACE)

The civilians were viewed as role models by 86% of the peers. Most of the women respected the dedication of the civilian staff and admired their goals, strength, and passion. The civilians in the program were not only able to provide the female peers with support, they were able to encourage the development of pro-social identities:

> "It was great. They gave me the inspiration to want to do more with my life. They made me see the good in myself, the good I didn't know I had." (Sky/CARE)

Ninety-eight percent of participants believed the peers and civilians were not only concerned with their success on the inside, they were also concerned with their ability to succeed upon release.

> "They wanted us to succeed. They had a vision of continuity... They wanted us to continue the work on the outside and they wanted us to be successful. I received letters of support from them. [supervisor's name] hooked me up with the only letter. They were proud of what we were doing." (W21/ACE)

> "We all cared about each other. We all want the other to succeed and go home. Regardless of what we are going through, we all want the best for one another. It is obvious that the civilian staff is very proud of those that left and are succeeding. We all cheer for each other. We would even cheer on for the civilian staff that was in school. We always want everyone to do well." (Rose/ACE)

All women involved with these programs felt as if the peer/civilian staff served as an extended family.

> "We mostly got along but there were times that we would argue and disagree. We ended up agreeing to disagree but we moved on. We all had strong opinions but we didn't stay mad for long." (Smarty/ACE)

> "Many of us are still great friends today. My closest and dearest friends are the women I had worked with in ACE. The younger members often came to me for guidance but I would not say that we were close friends because although they shared personal issues with me, I only shared with the older members." (Shyone/ACE)

> "We were very close, tight knit. I looked upon many of them as an extended family. Early on, most of us were long termers and we were at the beginning of our sentences. ACE was a safe place to go to share our struggles together." (Power/ACE & CARE)

> "It was beautiful. We really had a family and some of us were closer than others but we all had each other's back. There was no other place in prison with that type of unity." (Volcano/ACE)

Interviews indicated that the women felt that ACE/CARE were safe places, free from judgment.

> The majority of women were looking for a place where they would not be judged. I did not want to be judged either, so it went hand-in-hand. It was a place that we could all gather without having to worry that others were judging us. I was very welcomed by the ACE staff and we were very connected to one another. When one hurt, we all hurt. (January/ACE Peer)

Study participants not only valued the perceptions of their peers and the civilian staff, they valued the perceptions of the entire facility. In fact, being a role-model was espoused by a majority of the women and they were very cognizant of their behavior when on and off duty. They believed everything they did or did not do was not only a reflection of them, but of the entire program. It appeared that the perceptions of both inmate population and prison staff had an effect on how the women perceived themselves. These positive perceptions gave the women confidence and made them feel as if they were making a positive difference in the lives of others. As a result, 74% believed they were perceived differently than other inmates by prison staff because of their work in ACE/CARE. Over one-half of the sample (53%) thought that they were perceived as more dependable, more educated, more respected or more trustworthy than other inmates. They also felt they were perceived as role models and held to a higher standard than other inmates.

> "We were looked at as role models to others, to everybody." (Mary/ACE)

> "Everyone expected us to give it our all." (Compassionate/ACE)

> "We were there to do what we were supposed to do. The core group had high standards of work ethics. The core group actually ran like a board of directors." (Sarabanda/ACE)

> "I was perceived as someone who was serious and doing something meaningful. I was always respected. Except for one officer, I had no problems. I carried myself well and when I entered the units, they knew I was there to do my job. If I said I was going up there to counsel someone, they knew I was up there to counsel and that's it. They knew I wouldn't cause a problem." (Shak/CARE)

> "We had a lot of freedom. It was not a big deal to go on all of the housing units, to do the plays, or to carry all of our equipment around. There was a sense of being trusted. Think about just being on IPC at midnight. The COs completed trusted you and they would make positive comments about that. There was a great deal of respect. The superintendent even respected and admired us. Organizations on the outside were impressed with the work we were doing. In many instances, we had more services going on in ACE than most outside agencies had. It was a good feeling." (Purposed/ACE)

> "We were respected because we were doing something good for population. We gave them the information on how to take care of themselves. We were doing something positive for the community and dealing with really sensitive issues and I think that brought us a little more respect." (Mary/ACE)

Ninety-four percent stated they were also perceived differently by other inmates because of their work in ACE/CARE.

> "Yes, the peers saw me as someone who was knowledgeable and someone they could get clarity from. For the most part, I was well respected and they always called me Ms. [her last name], never by my first name. A few thought that I felt I was better than them but for the most part, I was someone who had information that could help them." (Shak/CARE)

> "Yes, it comes from the way our peers would treat us. It was common to get phone calls on the unit for someone who was having an emotional crisis. We would even get phone calls for women that weren't HIV positive. The officers would call for us to counsel other women before they would even make that call to OMH (Office of Mental health). The women asked for us, they respected us and they knew that we would keep everything confidential." (Purposed/ACE)

The conventional attachments to staff and peers, in addition to feelings of being viewed as role-models, aided in maintaining low disciplinary levels. If we define institutional success via disciplinary history, this group achieved high levels of institutional success. When interviewed, the peers stated that their disciplinary record was excellent (69%). Most did not perceive themselves to be a disciplinary problem (92%) and most did not think others perceived them as a disciplinary problem (86%). More than one-half (51%) of the peers had a decrease in the number of the tickets they received after joining ACE/CARE, while 47% experienced no change in rates of disciplinary infractions. Of the women who received infractions during their incarceration, only two stated that they did not believe that their decrease in infractions was related to their work in ACE/CARE. It should be noted that all of the women who did not experience a change in rates of problematic behavior were not disciplinary problems prior to seeking employment with ACE/CARE. For those that did experience a change, this reduction demonstrates that even the most problematic inmates are subject to behavior change when in a supportive environment.

Overall, the peers received 5.17 tickets prior to working for ACE/CARE and .95 tickets during the time they worked for ACE/CARE; most of these tickets were for minor to moderate rule violating behavior. A substantial decrease in tickets was incurred by this sample after employment with ACE/CARE and these differences proved to be statistically significant. On average, these women received less infractions than most other inmates in the United States (1 per year compared to 1.5 per year respectively) and less infractions than other female inmates in the United States (1 per year compared to two per year respectively) (Stephan, 1989)[2]. Overall, when utilizing a paired samples *t* test, the decrease in the rate of disciplinary infractions proved to be statistically significant (*t=2.918, df=46, two-tailed significance p=.005, 95% confidence interval=1.30 to 7.11*). The rate of keep-

[2]The Bureau of Justice Statistics did not have an updated study on national rates of disciplinary infractions, nor were they aware of one.

lock (i.e., being locked in one's cell for 23 out of 24 hours per day for disciplinary reasons) decreased substantially after an inmate began working for ACE/CARE and these results proved to be statistically significant (*t=2.289, df=19, two-tailed significance p=.034, 95% confidence interval .1627 to 3.6373*). These findings illustrate that there are correlating effects between working for an HIV prison-based peer education program and better institutional conduct. Twenty-two percent (n=11) of the women reported serving SHU (Special Housing Unit) time during their incarceration. SHU, which is strict solitary confinement, is located in a separate part of the facility at BHCF, and inmates are locked in a cell for 23 out of 24 hours a day and receive minimal to no privileges. Eight of these women served their SHU sentence(s) prior to working for ACE/CARE, one served a SHU sentence during the time she worked for ACE for having a fight with another inmate, and one inmate served a SHU sentence both before and during the time she was employed with ACE, which was also for fighting. Two women reported being placed in administrative segregation, but this was after they left the ACE Program.

Participation in ACE/CARE also impacted post-release success. Respondents were asked to give accounts of their most positive experiences in ACE/CARE; 67% of the women stated that it was the sense of community, trust, and support of the ACE/CARE staff. They wanted this support to continue upon release. All of the women interview said they relied or were planning to rely on ACE/CARE staff upon release. As one woman clearly noted:

> "… They called me a lot when I came home and that was important to me. ("69"/ACE/CARE Peer).

Emotional support was preferred from both inmate peers and civilians, but they relied heavily upon civilian staff for job assistance, recommendation letters, housing assistance, and assistance with parole. Strong social networks, coupled with high "social capital" is essential for successful female offender reintegration (Reisig et al., 2002). In this study, it was evident that the relationships with the peers and the civilian staff continued long after the women were discharged and these lasting relationships made an impact on the women's abilities to maintain conventional lifestyles. Ninety-two percent of the releasees were still in contact with their former ACE/CARE peer workers since their release and 75% remained in contact with the civilian staff.

Most of the releases were successful in their transition back to the community. Eighty-eight percent were working full-time at the time of the interview. In general, out of the 26 women that were released from prison after working for ACE/CARE, two returned to prison for a technical violation, awaiting release at the time of the interview, and one was rearrested for trespassing (i.e., trying to visit a friend in public housing) but was not sent back to prison. Therefore, the official recidivism rate for this population was 12% (n=3). When compared to official rates of recidivism nationally (Langan & Levin 2002), ACE/CARE peers had a much lower rate of recidivism when compared to all offenders released from American prison facilities (12% verses 44%). They were also less likely than other American female inmates to face additional prison time after release for either committing a new crime or for committing a parole violation (12% compared to 39.4% respectively) (Langan & Levin 2002). ACE/CARE peers had lower rates of recidivism than other female releasees in NYS. In 2002, 31% of women in NYS were returned to prison for parole violations (Staley, 2003), while only 8% of the ACE/CARE peers in the sample were returned. On average, the women were living at home approximately 5 years. Studies have found that after 5 years of release, the possibility of recidivating is extremely improbable (Human Rights Watch, 2002), therefore, the possibility of any of these women getting rearrested in the future seems highly unlikely.

DISCUSSION

This study demonstrates a link between nontraditional prison-based programming, like ACE/CARE, by reducing disciplinary infractions and recidivism, while cultivating strong networks of support to mitigate the process of prisonization. ACE/CARE peers were able to develop and maintain conventional roles. They were no longer identified by themselves or by others as merely *inmates*, they were role models. These two programs provided an unorthodox substitution for the traditional prison play family, cultivating strong, positive, prosocial relationships. They were successful in promoting conventional lifestyles and behavior, in addition to minimizing the pains of imprisonment for women. With the recent change in the nature (and diminishing numbers) of the prison play family, maladjustment is a concern (Propper, 1982). Although these relationships differed from the traditional play family, they paralleled many important characteristics (i.e., emotional support).

The current research shows that such supportive networks, which develop in prison, can prevent periods of maladjustment. ACE/CARE helped to promote institutional success by helping peers to maintain low disciplinary levels. A substantial decrease in tickets was incurred by this sample after employment with ACE/CARE and these differences proved to be statistically significant. On average, these women received less infractions than most other inmates in the United States (1 per year compared to 1.5 per year respectively) and less infractions than other female inmates in the United States (1 per year compared to two per year respectively) (Stephan, 1989). This finding illustrates that there are correlating effects between working for an HIV prison-based peer education program and better institutional conduct.

The women were able to adopt new conventional roles while incarcerated, create community, and have a system of support necessary to maintain those roles when released. The ACE/CARE family encouraged each peer to strive for success and the peers relied heavily upon such support and encouragement, especially after their release. Overall, peers had a very low rate of recidivism, particularly when compared to national rates of recidivism for other types of offenders.

The network of support created by participants protected the women from adopting many of the norms inherent in the traditional inmate subculture, it decreased their chances of prisonization, and it prevented maladjustment, which could have impacted the degree of prison infractions and rates of recidivism. These women served as role models and their new identities were supported and encouraged by their inmate coworkers and the ACE/CARE civilian staff. They were cognizant of the effect their behavior would have on the overall success of the program. For the most part, they were unwilling to engage in behavior that could result in prison disciplinary action; most were hesitant to jeopardize their position or to jeopardize the overall success of the program. Most wanted to live up to the expectations of their coworkers and most did not want to disappoint the ACE/CARE civilian staff. Although these women experienced high levels of stress while incarcerated and upon their discharge from prison, their relationships to each other served as a healthy outlet for emotional release. The women used ACE/CARE as a place to express themselves in an environment where they knew they would not be judged or stigmatized. If prison administrators and researchers are concerned about the problems associated with prisonization, providing female inmates with purposeful employment, in a supportive environment that cultivates conventional relationships, may be the answer.

LIMITATIONS

There are several limitations to the current study. First, the sample was not a random sample since it was an already established program within the prison. In an attempt to generalize findings to the population, demographics from the sample were compared to demographics for the entire incarcerated female population in NYS. Second, there was no true comparison or true control group in this study. Since the women in the sample were so diverse in terms of age, race, sentence length, crime, etc., it was not feasible to obtain another set of inmates or formerly incarcerated women that matched the sample groups' diverse attributes. It was also not feasible to have another group of inmates taken from their regularly scheduled programs to participate in a comparison group, as this would have disrupted the daily schedule of the prison facility. Rather, comparisons were made between groups. Third, self-reported data may not be the most reliable source of information (see Maxfield and Babbie, 1998).

CONCLUSION

This research helped to provide evidence that non-traditional programs, such as HIV prison-based peer programming, positively impact prison behavior, in addition to maintaining the larger purpose of increasing HIV/AIDS awareness among inmate population (Collica, 2002). It provides support for implementing such programming, even though most facilities are not utilizing them for educational or rehabilitative purposes. Previous findings indicated that only 18 states, just 20% of U.S. prisons, have an HIV prison-based peer program (Collica, 2007). Little research has been conducted on non-traditional prison-based programming; this study demonstrates that the same effects derived from traditional educational and vocational programming can be derived from non-traditional prison programming. In light of the results from this study, researchers should determine if other types of non-traditional prison programs afford inmates and prison administrators similar benefits. Researchers should focus on whether the same benefits for female inmates working in a HIV prison-based peer program can be achieved by male inmates in lieu of their dissimilar adjustment/coping strategies. Future research should also determine if there are other peer programs that create a sense of family and community within the prison environment.

Biography

Dr. Kimberly Collica-Cox is an Associate Professor in the Criminal Justice and Security Department with PACE University. Prior to teaching, Dr. Collica worked for a women's correctional facility in NYS coordinating an HIV prison-based peer education program and for a NY jail supervising their jail-based Transitional Services Unit. She trains professionals in HIV related issues in the NYS Metropolitan area and is a certified ACA (American Correctional Association) Auditor. Dr. Collica has a Ph.D. in Criminal Justice from the Graduate School and University Center of the City University of New York, a M.Phil from the Graduate School and University Center, a MA in Criminal Justice from John Jay College, and a BA in Criminology from John Jay College. Her research focus is female inmates, rehabilitation, reintegration issues surrounding HIV prison-based peer programming, and female correctional executives.

Acknowledgments

Special thanks to the New York State Department of Corrections and Community Supervision's Central Office Research Division and all of the ACE/CARE women, past and present. A sincere thank you to Dr. Gennifer Furst for reading an earlier version of this chapter.

References

Alarid,F. L., Burton, V. S., & Cullen, F. T. (2000). Gender and crime among offenders: Assessing the generality of social control and differential association theories. *Journal of Research in Crime and Delinquency, 37* (2),171-199.

Belknap, J. (2001). *The Invisible Women: Gender, Crime, and Justice* (2nd ed). Belmont, CA: Wadsworth.

Bonta, J., Pang, B., & Wallace-Capretta, S. (1995). Predicators of recidivism among incarcerated female offenders. *The Prison Journal, 75* (3), 277-294.

Canestrini, K. (1993). *Follow-up study of industrial training program participants 1993. N*ew York State Department Of Correctional Services.

Canter, R. (1982). Family correlates of male and female delinquency. *Criminology, 20* (2), 149- 167.

Cao, L., Zhao, J., & Van Dine, S. (1997). Prison disciplinary tickets: A test of the deprivation and importation models. *Journal of Criminal Justice, 25* (2), 103-113.

Casey-Acevedo, K., & Bakken, T. (2003). Women adjusting to prison: Disciplinary behavior and the characteristics of adjustment. *Journal of Health and Social Policy, 17* (4), 37-60.

Clemmer, Donald. 1940. *The Prison Community*. New York: Holt, Rinehart & Winston.

Collica-Cox, K. (2014). Counting Down: HIV Prison-Based Peer Education Programs and Their Connection to Reduced Disciplinary Infractions. *International Journal of Offender Therapy and Comparative Criminology, 58* (8), 931-952.

Collica, K. (2010). Surviving Incarceration: HIV Prison-Based Peer Programs Build Communities of Support for Female Offenders. *Deviant Behavior, 31* (4), 303-313.

Collica, K. (2007). The Prevalence of HIV Peer Programming in American Prisons: An Opportunity Wasted." *Journal of Correctional Health Care, 13* (4), 278-288.

Collica, K. (2002). Levels of Knowledge and Risk Perceptions about HIV/AIDS Among Female Inmates in New York State: Can Prison-Based HIV Programs Set The Stage for Behavior Change? *The Prison Journal, 82* (1), 101-123.

Correctional Educational Bulletin. (2002). National study reaffirms education reduces inmate recidivism. *Correctional Educational Bulletin, 5* (6).

Craddock, A. (1996). A comparative study of male and female prison misconduct careers. *The Prison Journal, 76*, 60-80.

Cranford, Susan and Rose Williams. 1998. "Critical issues in managing female offenders." *Corrections Today 60* (7):130-135.

Dalley, B. (1993). Following the rules? Women's responses to incarceration, New Zealand, 1880-1920. *Journal of Social History, 27* (2), 309-326.

DeBell, J. (2001). The female offender: Different…not difficult. *Corrections Today, 63* (1), 56-61.

Dobash, R., Dobash, R. E., & Gutteridge, S. (1986). *The imprisonment of women.* Basil Blackwell: New York.

Eaton, M. (1993). *Women after Prison*. Pennsylvania: Open University Press.

Enocksson, K. (1981). Correctional Programs: A review of the value of education and training in penal institutions. *Journal of offender Counseling, Services & Rehabilitation, 5, (*1), 5-18.

Fox, J. (1984). Women's prison policy, prisoner activism, and the impact of the contemporary feminist movement: A case study. *The Prison Journal, 64* (2),15-36.

Friedman, J., & Rosenbaum, D. (1988). Social control theory: The salience of components by age, gender, and type of crime. *Journal of Quantitative Criminology, 4* (4), 363-381.

Genders, E., & Player, E. (1990). Women lifers: Assessing the experience." *The Prison Journal, 70* (1), 46-57.

Gerber, J., & Fritsch, E. (1995). Adult academic and vocational correctional education programs. *Journal of Offender Rehabilitation, 22* (1/2), 119-142.

Giallombardo, R. (1966). *Society of Women*. New York: John Wiley & Sons, Inc.

Glaser, B., & Strauss, A. (1967). *Discovery of Grounded Theory: Strategies for Qualitative Research*. Chicago: Aldine.

Glaze, L., & Maruschak, L. M. (2010). *Parents in prison and their minor children. Bureau of Justice Statistics special report.* Washington, DC.: US Department of Justice.

Greenfeld, L., & Snell, T. (2000). Women Offenders. *Bureau of Justice Statistics Special Report*. Washington, DC.: US Department of Justice.

Greer, K. (2000). The changing nature of interpersonal relationships in a women's prison. *The Prison Journal, 80* (4), 442-468.

Glover, A. R., Perez, D. M., & Jennings, W. G. (2008). Gender differences in factors contributing to institutional misconduct. *The Prison Journal, 88* (3), 378-403.

Harer, M. (1995). *Prison education program participation: A test of the normalization Hypothesis*. Washington, DC.: Federal Bureau of Prisons Office of Research and Evaluation

Hewitt, J., Poole, E., & Regoli, R. (1984). Self-reported and observed rule breaking in prison: A look at disciplinary response. *Justice Quarterly*, 1 (3), 437-447.

Hirschi, T. (1969). *Causes of Delinquency*. Berkley: University of California Press.

Human Rights Watch. (2004). *No second chance: People with criminal records denied access to public housing*. New York: Human Rights

Watch. Retrieved from: http://www.hrw.org/sites/default/files /reports/ usa1104.pdf.

Humphrey, E. (1987). *Review of the literature on female security issues.* State of New York Department of Correctional Services Office of Classification

Irwin, J., & Cressey, D. (1962). Thieves, convicts, and the inmate culture." *Social Problems, 10* (2), 142-155.

Jiang, S. (2005). Impact of drug use on inmate misconduct: A multilevel analysis. *Journal of Criminal Justice, 33*, 153-163.

Jiang, S., & Winfree Jr., T. (2006). Social support, gender, and inmate adjustment to prison life. *The Prison Journal, 86* (1), 32-55.

Jones, R. (1993). Coping with separation: Adaptive responses of women prisoners. *Women and Criminal Justice, 5* (1), 71-97.

Koski, D. (1998). Vocational education in prison: Lack of consensus leading to inconsistent results. *Journal of Offender Rehabilitation 27,* (3/4), 151-164.

Koons, B., Burrow, J., Morash, M., & Bynum, T. (1997). Expert and offender perceptions of program elements linked to successful outcomes for incarcerated women." *Crime and Delinquency, 43* (4), 512-532.

Kruttschnitt, C. (2000). Doing her own time? *Criminology, 38* (3), 681-718.

Lasley, J. (1998). Toward a control theory of white-collar offending. *Journal of Quantitative Criminology, 4* (4), 347-362.

Linden, R. & Perry, L. (1982). The effectiveness of prison education programs. *Journal of Offender Counseling, Services & Rehabilitation, 6* (4), 43-57.

Linquist, C. (1980). Prison discipline and the female offender. *Journal of Offender Counseling, Services, and Rehabilitation,* 4 (4), 305-318.

Lahm, K. (2000). Equal or equitable: An exploration of educational and vocational Program availability for male. *Federal Probation*, 64 (2).

Langan, P. & Levin, D. (2002). Recidivism of Prisoners Released in 1994. Bureau of Justice Statistics Special Report. Washington, DC.: US Department of Justice.

MacKenzie, D. L., Robinson, J., & Campbell, C. (1989). Long-term incarceration of female offenders. *Criminal Justice and Behavior, 16* (2), 223-238.

Maxfield, M., & Babbie, E. (1998). *Research Methods For Criminal Justice and Criminology.* California: Wadsworth Publishing Company.

McClellan, D. (1994). Disparity in the discipline of male and female inmates in Texas prisons. *Women and Criminal Justice, 5* (2), 71-97.

MacDonald, D. (1995*). Overview of department follow-up research on return rates of participants in major programs 1995.* New York State Department of Correctional Services.

McCollum, S. (1994). Prison college programs. *The Prison Journal*, 73 (1), 51-61.

Miller, M. (1990). *Perceptions of available and needed programs by female offenders in Delaware*. Delaware Council on Crime and Justice.

Moyer, I. (1984). Deceptions and realities of life in women's prisons. *The Prison Journal, 64*, 45-56.

Nuttall, J., Hollmen, L., & Staley, M. (2003). The effect of earning a GED on recidivism rates. *Journal of Correctional Education, 54* (3), 90-94.

Owen, Barbara.. 1998. *In the mix: Struggle and survival in a woman's prison.* Albany: SUNY Press.

Parsons, M., & Warner-Robbins, C. (2002). Factors that support women's successful transition to the community following jail/prison. *Health Care For Women International 23* (1), 6-18.

Pollock-Byrne, J. (1990). *Women, Prison & Crime.* Pacific Grove, California: Brooks/Cole Publishing.

Propper, A. (1982). Make-believe families and homosexuality among imprisoned girls. *Criminology, 20* (1), 127-138.

Rankin, J. (1976). Investigating the interrelations among social control variables and conformity. *Journal of Criminal Law and Criminology, 67* (4), 740-480.

Reed, D., & Reed, E. (2004). Mothers in prison and their children. In *The Criminal Justice System & Women* (3rd ed) (ed. Price, B. & Sokoloff, N.). New York: McGraw Hill, 261-273.

Reisig, M., Holtfreter, K., & Morash, M. (2002). Social capital among women offenders. *Journal of Contemporary Criminal Justice, 18* (2), 167-187.

Rosenbaum, J. (1987). Social control, gender, and delinquency. *Justice Quarterly, 4* (1), 117- 132.

Sampson, R., & Laub, J. (1990). Crime and deviance over the life course: The salience of adult social bonds. *American Sociological Review, 55* (5), 609-627.

Schrum, H. (2004). No longer theory: Correctional practices that work. *The Journal of Correctional Education, 55* (3), 225-235.

Schumacker, R., Anderson, D., & Anderson, S. (1990). Vocational and academic indicators of parole success. *Journal of Correctional Education, 41* (1), 8- 13.

Severance, T. (2005). You know who you can go to: Cooperation and exchange between incarcerated women. *The Prison Journal, 85* (3), 343-367.

Shover, N., Norland, S., James, J., & Thornton, W. (1979). Gender roles and Delinquency. *Social Forces, 58* (1), 162-175.

Shover, N., & Thompson, C. (1992). Age, differential expectations, and crime. *Criminology, 30* (1), 89-104.

Smart, C. (1976). *Women, crime, and criminology: A feminist critique.* London: Routledge & Kegan Paul Ltd.

Stephan, J. (1989). *Prison rule violators. Bureau of Justice Statistics Special Report.* Washington DC: US Department of Justice.

Suter, J., Byrne, M., Byrne, S., Howells, K., & Day, A. (2002). Anger in prisoners: Women are different from men. *Personality and Individual Differences, 32* (6), 1087-1100.

Sykes, G., & Messinger, S. (1960). Inmate social systems. In *Theoretical Studies in social organization of the prison* (ed. Cloward, R.). New York: Social Science Research Council, 5- 19.

Snell, T., & Morton, D. (1994). *Women in prison: Survey of state inmates prison inmates, 1991. Bureau of Justice Statistics Special Report.* Washington, DC.: US Department of Justice.

Sommers, I., Baskin, D., & Fagan, J. (1994). Getting out of the life: Crime desistance by female street offenders. *Deviant Behavior, 15* (2), 125-149.

Staley, M. (2003). *Female Offenders: 2001-2002.* New York State Department of Correctional Services.

Taylor, J. (1992). Post-secondary correctional education: An evaluation of effectiveness and efficiency. *Journal of Correctional Education, 43* (3), 132-141.

Tewksbury, R. & Vito, G. (1994). Improving the educational skills of jail inmates: Preliminary program findings. *Federal Probation, 58* (2), 55-59.

Tischler, C., & Marquart, J. (1989). Analysis of disciplinary infraction rates among female and male inmates. *Journal of Criminal Justice, 17* (6), 507-513.

Tootoonchi, A. (1993). College education in prisons: The inmates' perspectives. *Federal Probation, 57* (4), 34-40.

Zaitzow, B. H, & Thomas, J. (2003). *Women in prison. Gender and Social control.* Colorado: Lynn Reiner Publishing.

In: Imprisonment and Incarceration
Editor: Hillary N. Clarkson
ISBN: 978-1-63482-117-9

Chapter 2

GLOBAL TRENDS IN INCARCERATION AROUND THE TURN OF THE 21ST CENTURY

Douglas B. Weiss *
California State University at San Bernardino, US

ABSTRACT

Since its initial publication in 1999, the World Prison Population List has documented an approximately 25% increase in the global prison population from more than 8 million incarcerated persons to more than 10.2 million as of October 2013. While substantial in absolute terms, this growth in incarceration may not be universal as three nations (United States, China, and Russia) have accounted for nearly half of the world's incarcerated population during this time. Due to this disproportionate representation, any changes in the incarcerated populations in these three nations would predominate changes in other nations. Indeed, incarceration growth over time is neither inevitable nor universal as evidenced by nations such as Finland which experienced a substantial decrease in the use of incarceration since the early 1950s. Using data from the International Centre for Prison Studies, this chapter explores global trends in incarceration and assesses the extent to which growth in incarceration was experienced throughout the world since the early 1990s. Special attention is given to trends in the composition of incarcerated populations in regards to remand and female prisoners.

*E-mail: dweiss@csusb.edu.

Several suggestions are made for future research on cross-national differences in incarceration use.

INTRODUCTION

Aside from capital punishment, incarceration represents the most severe and most costly punishment that state governments can administer to its citizens. The use of incarceration has garnered increasing attention over the years, particularly in the United States where incarcerated populations have undergone approximately forty years of nearly continuous growth. While the United States may be exceptional compared to the rest of the world in terms of the speed and extent of growth in incarceration, it is hardly the case that the United States is unique in experiencing incarceration growth over time. Since its initial publication in 1999, the World Prison Population List has documented an approximately 25% increase in the global prison population from more than 8 million incarcerated persons to more than 10.2 million as of 2013 (Walmsley, 2013).

While substantial in absolute terms, this growth is unlikely to be uniform as incarcerated populations are disproportionately distributed throughout the world. For instance, while the United States consists of 5% of the world population, it also accounts for 25% of the worlds' inmates (Walmsley, 2013). Along with China and Russia, these three nations account for about 45% of the prison population and about 26% of the global population. The disproportionate representation of these three nations in the global prison population has been documented for quite some time (Walmsley, 1999).

Due to their disproportionate representation, these three nations, particularly the United States, tend to receive an inordinate amount of attention in cross-national comparisons of incarceration. As a result, there is relatively less known about incarceration use in other nations throughout the world. Further, cross-national comparisons of incarceration are usually cross-sectional and compare rates in various nations at one particular point in time. In most cases, this comparison highlights the exceptionally high incarceration rate in the United States relative to other developed nations (e.g., Barclay and Tavares, 2003; Hartney, 2006; Mauer, 2003). Since these comparisons are cross-sectional, they are unable to address how nations' incarceration rates have changed over time. While U.S. incarceration rates are relatively high compared to most other nations, particularly developed nations, these sorts of comparisons do not capture whether a similar growth in incarceration has occurred in other nations.

This chapter seeks to address these gaps by exploring and describing incarceration trends worldwide using data from the International Centre for Prison Studies. The first section will describe the data that is being examined here and will highlight its limitations. The second section will examine regional and sub-regional trends in Africa, the Americas, Asia, Europe, and Oceania. The third and fourth sections will examine regional and sub-regional trends in two sub-groups that may be contributing to the worldwide growth in incarceration: remand and female prisoners, respectively. The fifth section will summarize these trends and offer suggestions for future research on cross-national studies of incarceration.

DATA

Overall Incarceration

Data for this chapter is taken from the World Prison Population List (WPPL) which has been published on an approximately biennial basis since 1999. The first five editions were published by the U.K. Home Office while the International Centre for Prison Studies has published every edition thereafter. The WPPL is the product of a compilation of a variety of data sources from nations throughout the world. Data sources include national prison administrations, the United Nations, the Council of Europe, the U.S. State Department, and NGOs such as Penal Reform International. The WPPL provides data on the total prison population for nations, the estimated national population, and the prison population rate which is calculated as the number of inmates per 100,000 national population.

There are several limitations to the WPPL due to the way in which data is collected. First, data is not available for all countries for all years. Since the years for which data is available differs across nations, it is not possible to include data for each year for each nation. In order to accommodate these differences and to maximize the number of nations included in the analysis, seven data waves were created with each wave representing a three-year interval (1993-1995, 1996-1998, 1999-2001, 2002-2004, 2005-2007, 2008-2010, 2011-2013). In most cases, data is available for nations during one of the three years within each wave. An average value was calculated in instances where nations had data available for more than one year within each wave.

An additional limitation to the WPPL is that different practices in different nations regarding whom is included in the prison population means that data is likely not directly comparable between nations. For instance, some nations may include juveniles in their prison population counts while other nations may exclude juveniles as they are held under a different jurisdiction. Other sub-groups that may or may not be included in prison population counts for different nations include pre-trial detainees, mentally ill offenders, and offenders detained for drug/alcohol problems (Walmsley, 2013). While these limitations prevent direct comparisons from being made across nations, data from the WPPL may still be considered informative of incarceration trends within nations.

Due to these limitations, several criteria were used to select nations for the sample being examined in this chapter. First, nations whose population was below 250,000 in 2000 were excluded from the analysis. Due to the small population sizes of these nations, any substantive changes to prison populations may result in dramatic increases or decreases in incarceration rates. Second, nations were excluded from the sample if they were missing data for three or more of the seven data waves available for overall incarceration rates.

Remand and Female Incarceration

In addition to the World Prison Population List, the International Centre for Prison Studies has published two editions of both the World Female Imprisonment List and the World Pre-trial/Remand Imprisonment list. Like the WPPL, data for these two publications are based on a compilation of different data sources. As a result, the data in these lists suffer from the same limitations as described above. While these two publications have shorter histories than the WPPL, both publications provide data on remand and female incarceration as far back as the early 2000s. Both publications provide data on imprisonment rates as well as the percentage of the prison population made up of each subgroup.

Since data is unavailable for all nations for all years, remand and female incarceration trends are based on four data waves composed of four years each (1999-2003, 2004-2007, 2008-2011, 2012-2014). For most nations, data was available for one year within each of the data waves and an average value was calculated for those waves in which data was available for multiple years within each wave. Nations were included in the analysis if data was available for at least three of the four waves and the nation had a population above 250,000 in 2000.

Global Incarceration Trends

Figure 1 presents the trend in the number of incarcerated persons worldwide as well as for the three nations with the largest incarcerated populations: the United States, China, and Russia. As can be seen, the global trend reflects a steady increase in the prison population from 1999 to 2013 and closely tracks the trends in the United States and China. Russia, on the other hand, has experienced a decrease in its prison population between 1999 and 2013.

Nevertheless, these three nations have retained the three largest national prison populations in the world during this period. Due to their disproportionate representation of the overall global prison population, the growth in these nations is likely responsible for the overall increase in the number of prisoners worldwide. The overall size of the prison population in these nations, however, may reflect the size of these national populations rather than the extent to which incarceration is used.

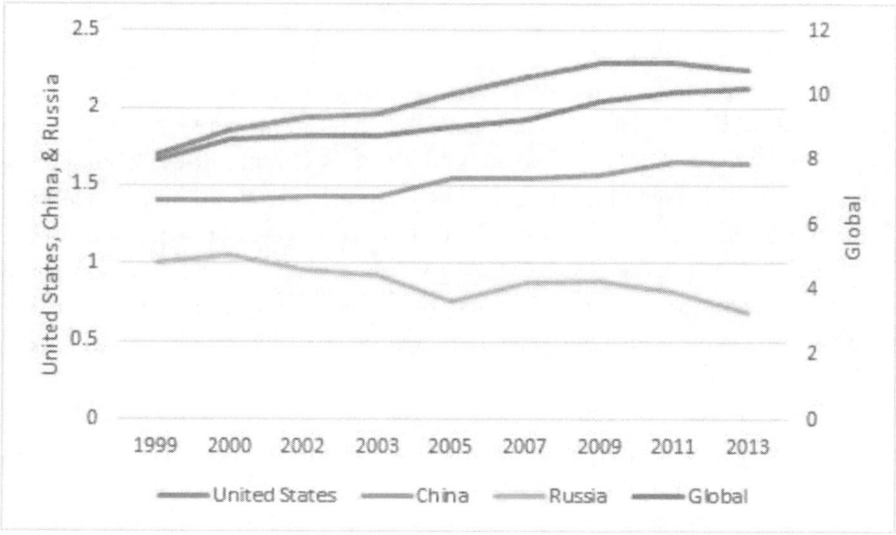

Figure 1. Total Prison Population (in Millions of prisoners): Global & Three Largest Nations.

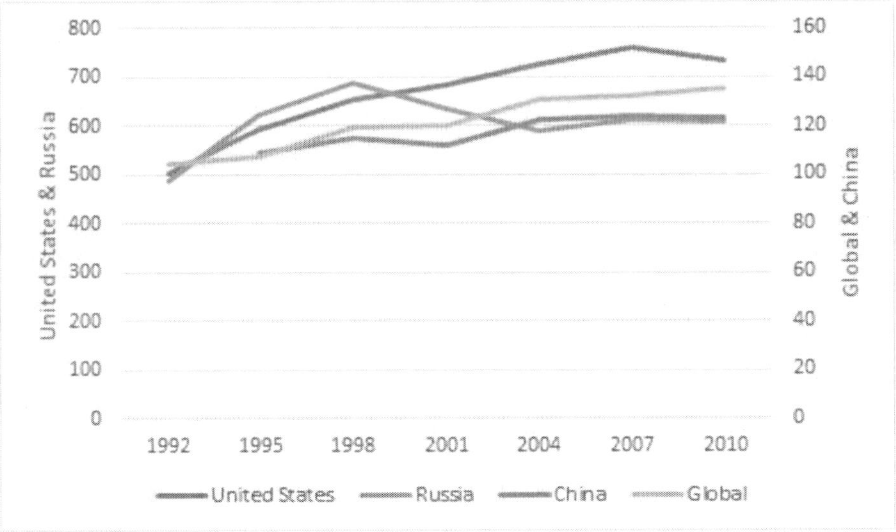

Figure 2. Worldwide & Three Largest Nations Incarceration Rates (per 100,000 population).

A better comparison would be national incarceration rates which account for differences in population size by measuring the number of prisoners per 100,000 population. Figure 2 depicts the trend in median incarceration rates for 176 nations as well as the national incarceration rates for the United States, China, and Russia. Two things are readily apparent from this figure. First, incarceration rates have increased worldwide as well as in these three nations since the early 1990s. This upward trend has been relatively steady with the exception of Russia where the incarceration rate is slightly down from a peak in the late 1990s. Second, there is considerable variation in the scale of incarceration rates as evidenced by the difference in rates between the United States and Russia, on the one hand, and China and the global median on the other. Incarceration rates in the United States and Russia are approximately five times as great as those in China and the global median.

The outlier status of the United States and Russia is further illustrated in Figure 3 which presents median incarceration rates across the regions of Asia, the Americas, Africa, Europe and Oceania. During the early 1990s, median incarceration rates in these regions were similar in magnitude at around 100 inmates per 100,000 population. While most of the regions have maintained relatively stable median incarceration rates over the past twenty years, the median incarceration rate for the Americas has increased over time such that the median rate around 2010 was nearly twice as great as in the early 1990s.

Since median incarceration rates are not susceptible to outliers such as the United States, it appears that incarceration growth is particularly pronounced in the Americas.

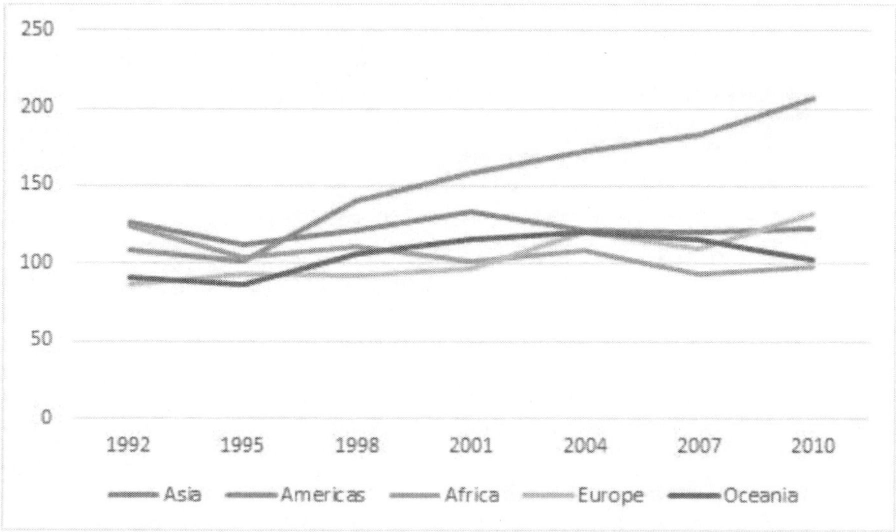

Figure 3. Regional Median Incarceration Rates (prisoners per 100k population).

An examination of incarceration trends across global regions, however, fails to capture within-region variability which may be substantial in many cases. Figure 4 depicts within-region variability in incarceration trends across four regions: Africa, the Americas, Asia, and Europe[1]. This figure reveals some of that sub-regional variability and illustrates how median incarceration are almost consistently greater in some regions than others. For instance, panel A indicates median incarceration rates in the Southern Africa region are consistently greater than those in other regions during the observation period. Panels B-D are also similar in that the median incarceration rates in North America, Central Asia, Eurasia, and Eastern Europe tend to be greater than those in its relative sub-regions.

Panel A presents trends in median incarceration rates throughout five African sub-regions: North, South, East, West, and Central. Whereas median incarceration rates in North, East and Central African nations are relatively similar, incarceration rates in South and West African nations appear to be

[1]Oceania is treated as one whole region and, as such, is not included in the discussion of sub-regional trends.

clearly distinct as the highest and lowest, respectively, in the region. Although this respective positioning was maintained throughout the observation period, increases in incarceration rates were observed throughout Africa. The greatest increase in incarceration rates was observed in North Africa where the median incarceration rate was 56% greater around 2010 than the early 1990s. Although East and West African nations also experienced an increase in incarceration during the observation period, the change in these nations was modest in comparison.

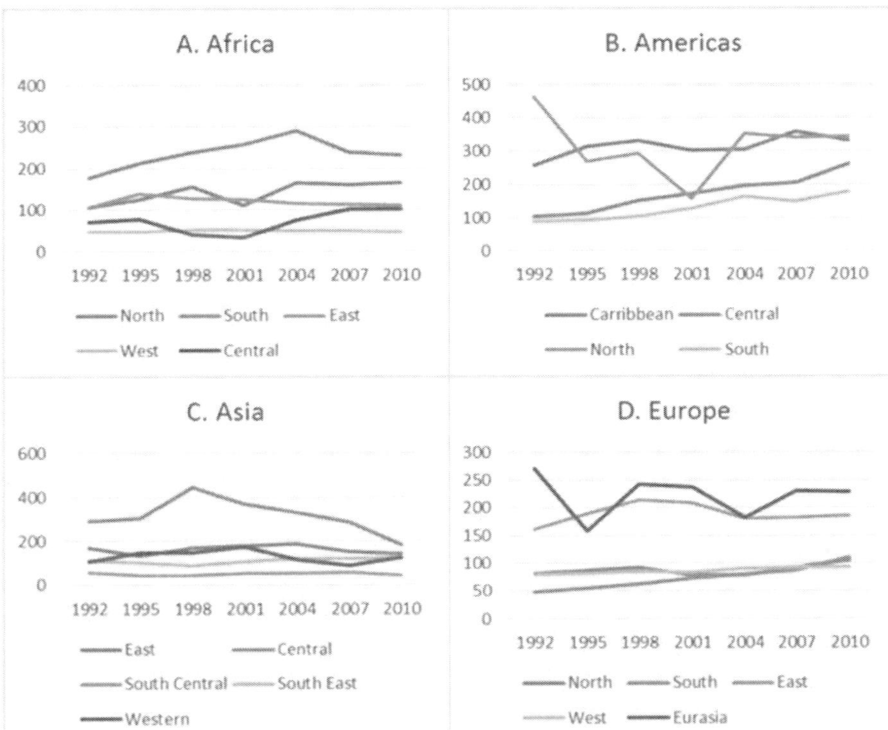

Figure 4. Sub-Regional Median Incarceration Rates (prisoners per 100k population).

Panel B illustrates trends in median incarceration rates in four American sub-regions: the Caribbean, Central, North, and South America. In this region, median incarceration rates in the Caribbean and North America were consistently greater than those in Central and South America, although the gap between these nations has decreased over time. Median incarceration rates in Central and South America increased by 150% and 100%, respectively, between the early 1990s and the end of the observation period. While the

United States garners much attention for its growth in the use of incarceration, it appears that increased use of incarceration has been a trend common throughout each of the sub-regions in the Americas.

Panel C depicts sub-regional variability in incarceration trends in five Asian regions: East, Central, South Central, South East, and Western Asia. With the exception of Central Asia, trends in median incarceration rates across East, South Central, South East and Western Asia have remained relatively stable and at a similar level throughout the observation period. Central Asian nations had the highest incarceration rates throughout the entire observation period, although there was a substantial decline in incarceration in this region beginning around the late 1990s, such that the incarceration rate for this region more closely resembled the rates observed in the rest of the Asian sub-regions. South Central and East Asian regions also experienced a decline in median incarceration rates during the observation period.

Panel D provides sub-regional trends in median incarceration rates in five European regions: North, South, East, West, and Eurasia. This figure suggests median incarceration rates in Europe roughly fall into two groups that follow geographic lines: a group consisting of the Eastern European and Eurasian sub-regions where median incarceration rates are high and a group consisting of Northern, Southern, and Western Europe where median incarceration rates are relatively low. Although median incarceration rates were similar in North, South, and West Europe, Southern European nations experienced a substantial 141% increase in its median incarceration rate between the early 1990s and the end of the observation period. Despite this increase, the median incarceration rate in Southern Europe remained similar to that of Northern and Western Europe due to the relatively low rates in this region in the early 1990s.

Altogether, median incarceration rates rose in most of the worlds' regions and sub-regions from the early 1990s through the beginning of the 21st century. Although all sub-regions in the Americas and Africa experienced an increase in median incarceration rates during this time, the growth in incarceration was most apparent in the Americas. Although significant attention has been given to the growth in incarceration in the United States due to its speed and magnitude, it would appear that incarceration growth is particularly pronounced throughout the Americas compared to the rest of the world.

Although median incarceration rates rose throughout most of the world around the turn of the 21st century, there were several regions that experienced substantial declines in incarceration during this time. The most substantial declines were observed in the regions of Central, South Central, and East Asia.

Median incarceration rates also declined in the Eurasian sub-region, although they remain high relative to other European sub-regions. An examination of the factors driving these trends is beyond the scope of this chapter, although it is a subject that is worthy of further exploration.

Finally, there appears to be a convergence in median incarceration rates over time in most of the world's regions although there is still a considerable gap between the sub-regions within each global region. This is most apparent in the Americas and Asia and in Europe to a lesser extent. In the Americas, median incarceration rates are rising in the Central and South sub-regions to the higher rates observed in the Caribbean and North America. Median incarceration rates in Southern, Western, and Northern Europe are also increasing faster relative to Eastern Europe and Eurasia, although a sizable gap still remains. The opposite trend is observed in Asia where the relatively high rates in Central Asia have declined over time to a lower level that is observed throughout the rest of Asia. The only region that hasn't experienced convergence in sub-regional median incarceration rates over time is Africa where a considerable gap remains between the sub-regions with the highest and lowest median rates.

Global Trends in the Composition of Incarcerated Populations

While the preceding section described trends in how median incarceration rates have changed throughout the world around the turn of the 21st century, these trends fails to capture whether, and, if so, how the composition of incarcerated populations may have changed during this time. In addition to data on overall incarceration trends, the international Centre for Prison Studies provides data on two sub-groups of inmates: remand and female prisoners. This section explores trends in the incarceration of remand and female prisoners in terms of both rates and the percentage of incarcerated populations that are made up of these two subgroups.

REMAND PRISONERS

The use of incarceration for remand is problematic as these individuals are innocent and have yet to be proven guilty in a court of law. A recent report by the Open Society Institute documents the many problems faced by remand prisoners throughout the world (Schonteich, 2014). Figure 5 displays trends in remand incarceration in terms of both the remand incarceration rate as well as the percentage of the incarcerated population that is made up of remand prisoners in each of the five global regions. The two panels in this figure reveal two different patterns regarding the use of remand incarceration depending on how it is measured.

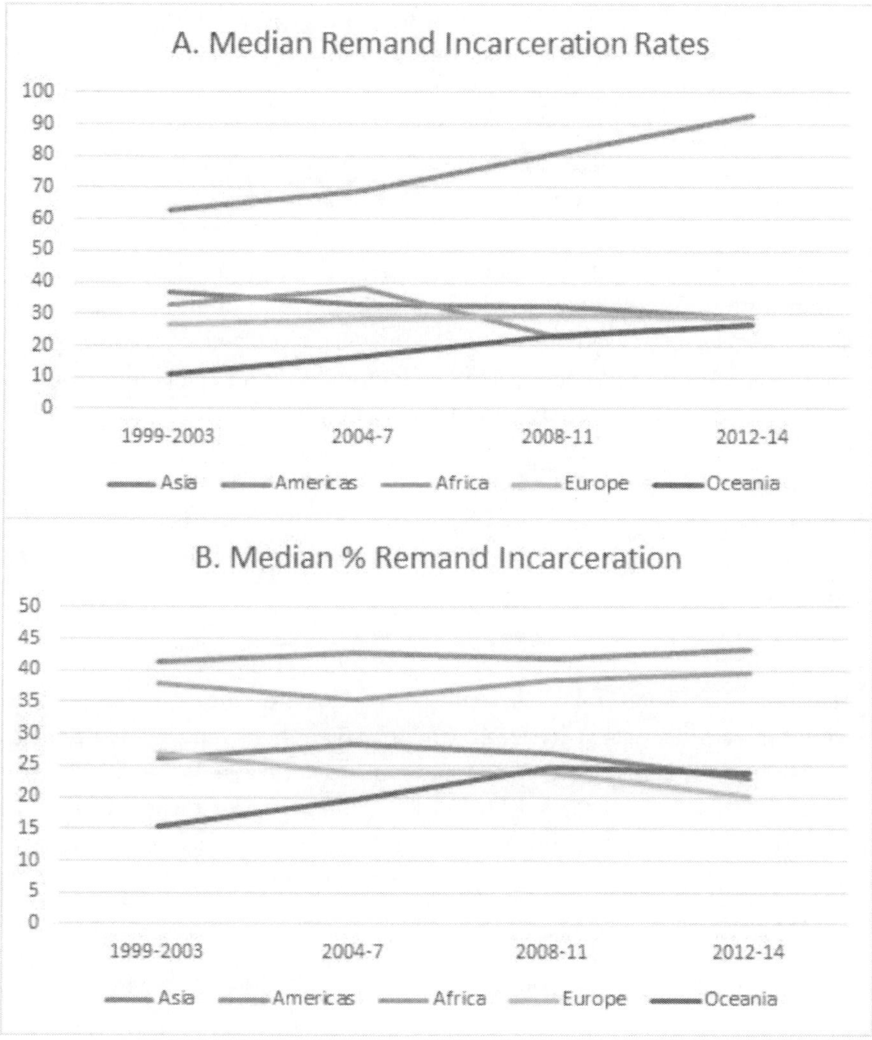

Figure 5. Regional Median Remand Incarceration.

Panel A shows the median remand incarceration rate in the Americas has increased during the beginning of the 21st century to a level that is about four times as great as that in any other of the world's regions. Similar to the the trend observed for overall median incarceration rates, the median remand imprisonment rate in the Americas is increasing much faster relative to the other four regions which have maintained relatively stable median incarceration rates and which have also converged over time.

In contrast, Panel B shows the highest median remand percentages are observed in Africa and Americas. Approximately 40% of the incarcerated populations in these regions are composed of remand prisoners. Both of these regions also experienced an approximately 4% increase in the percentage of the incarcerated population that is composed of remand prisoners between the first and last wave. While African prisons are composed of a similar percentage of remand prisoners as the Americas, Africa's median remand imprisonment rate is much closer to that observed in Asia, Europe, and Oceania as shown in Panel A. Aside from these two regions, Oceania was the only other region in which the percentage of the prison population made up of remand prisoners increased during this time. The percentage of the prison populations made up of remand prisoners declined in both Asia and Europe by 11% and 25%, respectively, between the first and last wave.

Figure 6 presents sub-regional trends in remand incarceration rates as well as the percentage of incarcerated populations made up of remand inmates for each of the four global regions. As observed in Figure 5, the pattern in the use of remand incarceration differs on whether incarceration rates or percentages are considered.

Panel A shows median remand incarceration rates throughout Africa have converged during the beginning of the 21st century. This convergence is most apparent in the South African sub-region where the median remand incarceration rate decreased by approximately 60% between the first and last waves. Median remand incarceration rates in Eastern and Western Africa in 2014 are also lower than rates in the early 2000s. Unlike these sub-regions, median remand incarceration rates increased by approximately 70% during the observation period in North Africa which currently has the highest rate in the African region.

While remand incarceration rates have converged over time in each of the African sub-regions, Panel B shows there are still differences between the African sub-regions in terms of the percentage of incarcerated populations made up of remand prisoners. The highest rates are found in East and West Africa where the median percentage of incarcerated populations made up of remand prisoners is around 40%. The median percentage for North Africa was also around 40% at the beginning of the observation period, although it has since declined to around 20% which is similar to the level in South Africa.

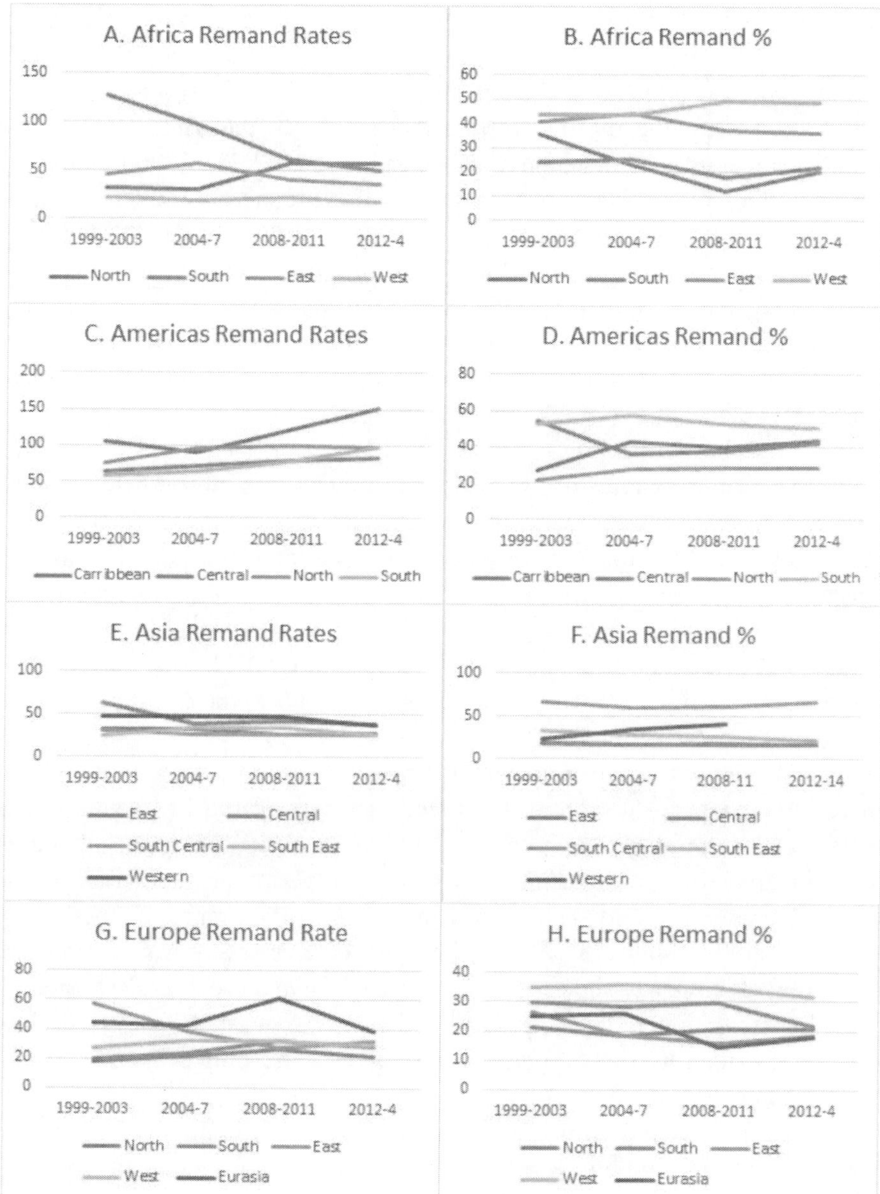

Figure 6. Sub-Regional Median Remand Incarceration (prisoners per 100k population).

Panel C indicates an upward trend in median remand incarceration rates in each of the four sub-regions in the Americas. The most substantial increase was in South America where the median remand incarceration rate in the most recent wave was approximately 70% greater than the rate in the first wave. The Caribbean has maintained the regions' highest median remand incarceration rate with the exception during the mid-2000s where it dropped slightly lower than the rate in North America. Since that time, the median remand incarceration rate in the Caribbean has increased by approximately 66% while the rate in North America has remained relatively stable. Although median remand incarceration rates in North America have remained relatively stable since the mid-2000s, the median rate in North America is about 28% higher in the final wave than at the initial wave. Median remand incarceration rates in Central America increased by a similar margin during this time.

A slightly different picture emerges in Panel D which shows trends in the median percentage of the prison population composed of remand prisoners in the four sub-regions in the Americas. While the Caribbean had the highest median imprisonment rate in the Americas and has experienced the greatest increase, the median percentage in the Americas has been relatively stable since the mid-2000s and is quite similar to that of Central America. The highest median percentage in the Americas is found in South America where approximately 50% of the incarcerated population is composed of remand prisoners. The median percentage in North Americas' prisons made up of remand prisoners has remained relatively stable at between 20-30% since the beginning of the 21st century.

Panel E shows median remand incarceration rates in each of the Asian sub-regions appear to have converged since the turn of the 21st century. The Western and Central Asian regions which maintained the highest median remand incarceration rates during the observation period also experienced the greatest decreases. While median remand incarceration rates in these sub-regions are still the highest in Africa, the most recent rates in these regions are now at a level similar to those of other African regions around 2000. Median remand incarceration rates in Eastern and South Central Asia also slightly decreased during this time. South East Asia was the only region in which median remand incarceration rates did not decrease. The median rate in this region increased by approximately 10% between the beginning and end of the observation period although it remains at a level similar to that of East and South Central Asia.

Even though median remand incarceration rates have converged during the beginning of the 21st century, Panel F shows the South Central Asian sub-region has a substantially larger proportion of their prison population made up of remand prisoners compared to the rest of the Asian sub-regions. During the beginning of the 21st century, approximately 70% of inmates in South Central Asian prisons were being held for remand. This is substantially greater than the approximately 20% of the prison populations of East, Central, and South East Asian prisons composed of remand prisoners.

Panel G shows median remand incarceration rates in each of the European subregions have converged over time. The median remand incarceration rates in Eastern Europe and Eurasia were two to three times as great as other European regions around 2000. Approximately fifteen years later, median remand incarceration rates in these regions declined to around 35 prisoners per 100,000 population. This level is more in line with the rest of Europe although these two regions continue to maintain the highest median remand incarceration rates in the region. Median remand incarceration rates in the other European sub-regions increased during the beginning of the 21st century with Southern Europe reporting the greatest increase (40%) followed by the Northern (22%) and Western (7%) regions.

Panel H shows that the median percentage of prison populations in the European sub-regions has converged over time with the exception of Western Europe which remains an outlier. The proportion of Western European prisons composed of remand prisoners has maintained relatively stable around 30-35% while the equivalent value for the other European sub-regions has hovered around 20%.

In sum, trends in remand incarceration differ depending on whether one considers the remand imprisonment rate or the percentage of the incarcerated population made up of remand prisoners. Median remand incarceration rates have converged among four of the five global regions with the exception of the Americas which has a rate several times greater than the other regions. Median remand incarceration rates have also converged within most regions with the exception of the Americas where the growth in the Caribbean rate has outpaced that of the other American sub-regions. In contrast, there has been no convergence either among regions or within regions in the percentage of incarcerated populations made up of remand prisoners.

FEMALE INCARCERATION

Another possible contributor to the growth in incarceration is an increase in the number of female prisoners. While males account for an overwhelming majority of criminal offending and prison populations throughout the world, female incarceration rates are rising in most nations. Further, this growth is often occurring at a pace faster than the male incarceration rate which means that females are making up an increasing share of incarcerated populations worldwide. Despite the growth of females outpacing that of males, however, the proportion of incarcerated populations that are made up of females is still relatively small.

Between 2006 and 2012, the number of female prisoners worldwide has increased by approximately 25% from approximately half a million to more than 625,000 women and girls (Walmsley, 2006, 2012). As for overall prison population worldwide, the nations of the United States, China, and Russia account for a disproportionate part of this population holding roughly one-third of the number of women and girls incarcerated worldwide.

Figure 7 illustrates regional trends in median female incarceration rates and the percentage of the incarcerated populations composed of females in each of the five global regions since the beginning of the 21st century. Panel A shows that median female incarceration rates have increased in most of the world's regions during this time. As observed for remand incarceration, the Americas region has maintained the highest median female incarceration rate since the turn of the century. The median female incarceration rate in the Americas has increased by approximately 50% between the initial and final waves which is similar to the increase in remand incarceration for this region. As observed for remand incarceration, the largest increase in median female incarceration rates is found in Oceania. During the beginning of the 21st century, the median female incarceration rate in Oceania nearly doubled and currently has the second highest percentage among the five regions.

Median female incarceration rates also increased in the Asian and European regions at the beginning of the 21st century. The increase in median female incarceration rates during the observation period in these regions was relatively similar although it was slightly larger in Asia (47%) than Europe (38%). The only region in which median female incarceration rates did not increase was Africa which has maintained the lowest median female incarceration rates throughout the observation period.

Panel B presents the median percentage of incarcerated populations made up of females for each of the five regions. During the beginning of the 21st century, females made up an increasing proportion of incarcerated populations in each global region with the exception of Africa. The largest increases were observed in Oceania and Asia where the percentage of females that make up the incarcerated population increased by 98% and 43% respectively. Despite these substantial increases over time, females made up no more than 7% of incarcerated populations in each of the world's regions.

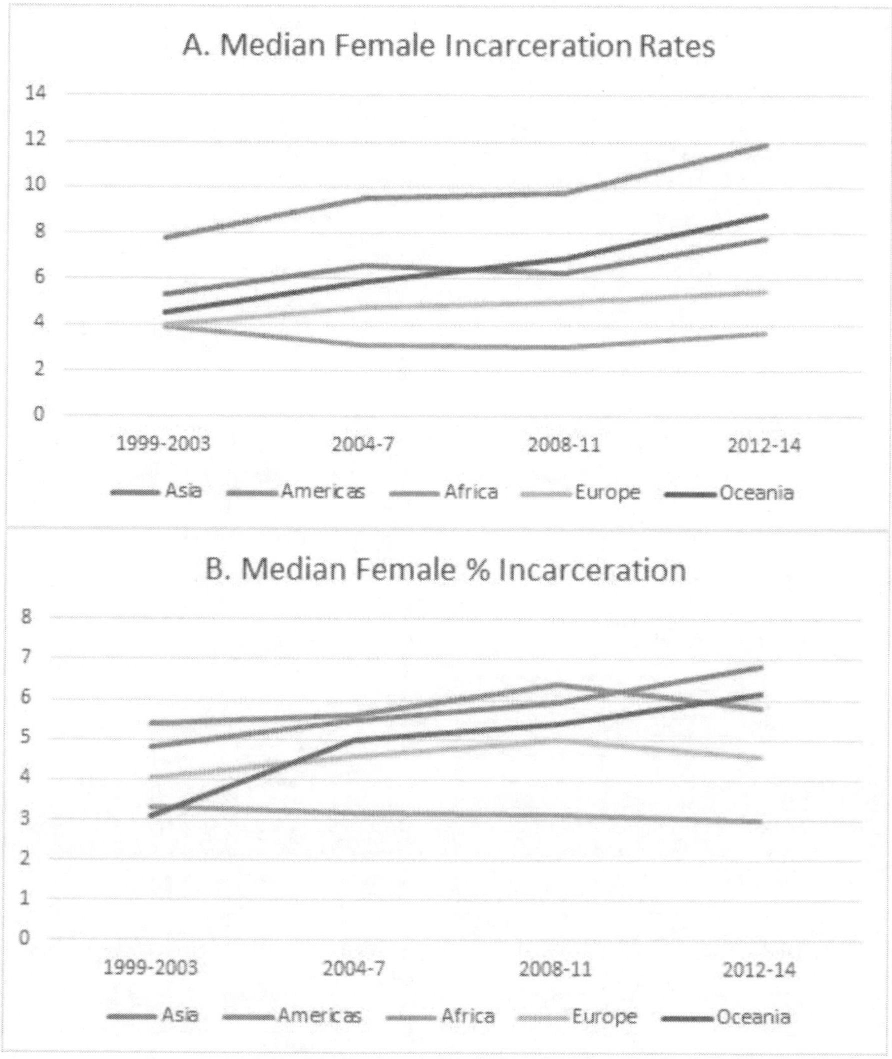

Figure 7. Regional Median Female Incarceration.

Figure 8 presents sub-regional trends in median female incarceration rates and the percentage of incarcerated populations made up of females in the regions of Africa, the Americas, Asia, and Europe. As observed for remand incarceration, the trends differ depending on whether incarceration rates or percentages are considered.

Figure 8. Sub-Regional Median Female Incarceration.

Panel A shows that there has been some convergence in median female incarceration rates in the four African sub-regions although a sizable gap remains between the sub-regions with the highest and lowest median rates. Median female incarceration rates were greatest in Southern Africa throughout the observation period although the rate for this region declined by 24% between the initial and final waves. The median female incarceration rate in Northern Africa dropped by an even larger 60% between these waves; a drop which is nearly entirely attributable to the decrease that occurred in Libya from seven female prisoners per 100,000 population around the mid-2000s to about one at the end of the observation period. Median female incarceration rates remained relatively stable in Eastern and Western Africa throughout this time around rates of four and one prisoners per 100,000 population, respectively.

Panel B shows sub-regional trends in female incarceration are mixed with females making up an increasing share of the prison populations in the East and West African sub-regions while declining in Northern and Southern Africa. Regardless of the change over time, females make up no more than 5% of the prison population in any of the African sub-regions which is the lowest percentage relative to any of the other worlds' regions.

Panel C indicates median female incarceration rates have trended upward in each of the four American sub-regions during the beginning of the 21st century. The greatest increase occurred for South and Central America where median female incarceration rates rose by 71% and 64%, respectively, between the initial and most recent wave. North America experienced a smaller increase of 15% in median female incarceration rates during this time. Nevertheless, North America (which in this case only includes the United States due to a lack of data for Canada) has maintained a female incarceration rate that is between 5-7 times as great as other sub-regions in the Americas. After an upward trend during the 2000s, median female incarceration rates in the Caribbean have declined in recent years to a rate that is similar to its rate in the early 2000s.

Panel D presents sub-regional trends in the Americas for the percentage of incarcerated populations made up of females. With the exception of the Caribbean, the female make-up of prisons in each of the sub-regions in the Americas increased by approximately 10% between the initial and most recent waves. Although North America, which again consists of the United States only, is the sub-region with the largest proportion of females incarcerated, the largest percentage may be found in the nation of Bolivia. Although Bolivia is an outlier relative to other South American countries, there has been a substantial decrease during the beginning of the 21st century in the percentage of its prison population who are female. Both Central and South America experienced similar trends in female incarceration which increased from 1999 to a peak around 2008-2011 and a slight decline since then.

Panel E shows that median female incarceration rates have trended upward during the beginning of the 21st century for most of the Asian sub-regions. The most substantial increases occurred in South Central, South East, and East Asia where the median female incarceration rate rose between the initial and final waves by 62%, 85%, and 38% respectively. Despite the considerable increase in South Central Asia, the median female incarceration rate in this region remains the lowest relative to the other Asian sub-regions. Median female incarceration rates remained relatively stable during the observation period in Central and Western Asia.

Panel F illustrates sub-regional trends in the percentage of the incarcerated populations made up by females in the five Asian sub-regions. During the beginning of the 21st century, females made up an increasing share of prison populations in each sub-region within Asia with the exception of the South Central region where the median percentage remained relatively stable. The greatest increase was observed in the Middle East where the median percentage of the prison population made up of females nearly doubled during the beginning of the 21st century. The two Asian sub-regions with the largest percentages of female inmates, East and South-East Asia, also experienced substantial increases during this time.

Panel G shows median female incarceration rates increased throughout each of the five European sub-regions. The Southern European and the Eurasian sub-regions experienced the greatest increases in median female incarceration rates. During the observation period, median female incarceration rates more than doubled in Southern Europe (2 to 4.4 prisoners per 100,000 population) and nearly doubled in Eurasia (4 to 7.2). The next greatest increase was in Northern Europe where the median female incarceration rate increased by 24% during this time. Eastern Europe, which has the highest median female incarceration rates in Europe, experienced an increase similar in magnitude. Median female incarceration rates remained relatively stable in Western Europe around 4.5 female prisoners per 100,000 population.

Sub-regional trends in the percentage of incarcerated populations made up of females are depicted in Panel H. Females made up an increasing share of prison populations throughout Europe during the beginning of the 21st century with the exception of Western Europe where the trend in female incarceration remained relatively stable. The largest increase is found in Eurasia where the median percentage increased by approximately 42% between 1999 and 2014. Despite this increase, Eurasia still maintained the lowest median percentage of female incarceration in Europe during the past fifteen years. Approximately 5% of the prison populations in the Northern, Eastern, and Western European sub-regions were female.

In sum, female incarceration rates and the percentage of incarcerated populations composed of females have increased throughout most of the world, although there is variation in the trends in these two measures within each region. Despite this growth, females still make up a considerably smaller proportion of incarcerated populations worldwide.

SUMMARY AND DISCUSSION

This chapter sought to describe worldwide trends in incarceration use around the turn of the 21st century with special attention being given to trends in remand and female incarceration. It is apparent that there are clear differences in incarceration use across global regions as well as within regions. While a description of these trends is enlightening in its own right, it is hoped this descriptive study may be used to inform future explanatory studies of cross-national differences in overall incarceration as well as in remand and female incarceration.

Several patterns in incarceration use emerged from this descriptive study. First, there appears to be a convergence in median incarceration rates across the regions of Africa, Asia, Europe, and Oceania as well as within these regions. The gap in median incarceration rates across these regions as well as within them was smaller at the end of the first decade of the 21st century than it was at the turn of the century. A similar pattern was observed for median remand incarceration rates for each of these four regions. The only region which didn't experience convergence in either overall incarceration or remand incarceration was the Americas where growth in these median rates has outpaced that of other regions.

Another pattern that emerged was that different trends emerged in remand and female incarceration depending on whether rates or the percentage composition of incarcerated populations was being considered. For instance, while the median remand incarceration rate in the Americas grew several times faster than that of other regions, the percentage of the incarcerated population in the Americas made up of remand prisoners remained relatively stable at a level similar to that in Africa during the beginning of the 21st century. Although there have been few cross-national investigations of remand or female incarceration to date, future studies should give careful consideration to which measure (rate or percentage) would be most appropriate for the particular research question being addressed.

Thus far, cross-national studies on incarceration use has largely been a piecemeal enterprise in which the relationship between incarceration rates and specific social, economic, and/or political factors have been investigated (e.g., Lappi-Seppala, 2011). While these studies have identified several possible relationships, there still lacks an overarching theory of punishment which attempts to incorporate each of this different factors in its explanatory framework. Future research on cross-national differences in incarceration should continue to explore potential relationships between incarceration rates and various factors with special focus being given to explaining change in incarceration use over time. For instance, one potential research question might examine why sub-regional incarceration rates appear to have converged over time.

Additionally, existing research on cross-national differences in incarceration has focused exclusively on overall incarceration rates and has neglected to investigate factors associated with changes in the composition of incarcerated populations including both remand and female prisoners. While remand imprisonment may be due to changes in policies concerning incarceration use across nations, it would be worthwhile for future studies to investigate possible relationships between social, economic, or demographic factors, on one hand, and the use of remand incarceration on the other.

Future studies should also further explore cross-national differences in female incarceration. Increasing trends in female incarceration rates as well as in the proportion of incarcerated populations that are made up of females may reflect two possibilities. First, it could be an indication that females have become increasingly involved in crime over time. Increased criminal offending will result in a greater number of females being arrested, convicted, and incarcerated. Policy changes may also increase the number of females who are incarcerated. For instance, Bloom, Chesney-Lind, and Owen (1994) find the War on Drugs in the United States had a disproportionate impact on women and contributed to the increased numbers of females in prison populations.

Alternatively, female incarceration may be increasing because their treatment in criminal justice systems around the world has become more similar to the ways in which males are sanctioned by the justice system. Thus, it might be expected that female incarceration may be greater in societies marked by greater gender equality and less patriarchy. Questions regarding female incarceration have only begun to receive attention at the cross-national level (e.g., Kruttschnitt et al., 2011).

Finally, future cross-national research on incarceration trends should consider the use of advanced longitudinal data methods. Advanced methods such as semi-parametric group-based trajectory modeling (Nagin, 2005) or growth curve modeling (Duncan, Duncan, and Stryker, 2013) have primarily been used to study individual development in offending although such methods are being increasingly applied to study crime at the macro level. These methods could provide insight into a number of questions related to international trends in incarceration such as whether there are "groups" of nations that demonstrate distinctive incarceration trends or address what factors drive initial incarceration rates as well as change over time.

References

Barclay, G., and Tavares, C. 2003. *International comparisons of criminal justice statistics* 2001. Home Office: London.

Bloom, B.,Chesney-Lind, M., and Owen, B. 1994. Women in California prisons: Hidden victims of the war on Drugs. *The Center on Juvenile and Criminal Justice*: San Francisco.

Duncan, T.E., Duncan, S.C., and Stryker, L.A. 2013. *An introduction to latent variable growth curve modeling:* Concepts, issues, and Applications, 2nd ed.

Hartney, C. 2006. US rates of incarceration: *A global perspective. National Council on Crime and Delinquency:* Washington, D.C.

International Centre for Prison Studies, World Prison Brief. Retrieved Decemeber 20, 2014 at http://www.prisonstudies.org/info/worldbrief.

Kruttschnitt, C., Slotboom, A-M., Dirkzwager, A., and Bijleveld, C. 2011. Bringing women's carceral experiences into the "new punitiveness" fray. Justice Quarterly, 30(1), 18-43.

Lappi-Seppala, T. 2011. Explaining imprisonment in Europe. European Journal of Criminology, 8(4), 303-328.

Mauer, M. 2003. Comparative international rates of incarceration: An examination of causes and trends. Washington, DC: The Sentencing Project.

Schonteich, M. 2014. Presumption of guilt: The global overuse of pretrial detention. Open Society Foundations: New York.

Walmsley, R. 1999. World prison population list, 1st ed. Home Office: London.

Walmsley, R. 2000. World prison population list, 2nd ed. Home Office: London.

Walmsley, R. 2002. World prison population list, 3rd ed. Home Office: London.

Walmsley, R. 2003. Global incarceration and prison trends. Forum on Crime and Society, 3(1&2), 65-78.

Walmsley, R. 2003. World prison population list, 4th ed. Home Office: London.

Walmsley, R. 2003. World prison population list, 5th ed. Home Office: London.

Walmsley, R. 2005. World prison population list, 6th ed. International Centre for Prison Studies: London.

Walmsley, R. 2006. World female imprisonment list, 1st ed. International Centre for Prison Studies: London.

Walmsley, R. 2007. World prison population list, 7th ed. International Centre for Prison Studies: London.

Walmsley, R. 2008. World pre-trial/remand imprisonment list, 1st ed. International Centre for Prison Studies: London.

Walmsley, R. 2009. World prison population list, 8th ed. International Centre for Prison Studies: London.

Walmsley, R. 2011. World prison population list, 9th ed. International Centre for Prison Studies: London.

Walmsley, R. 2012. World female imprisonment list, 2nd ed. International Centre for Prison Studies: London.

Walmsley, R. 2013. World prison population list, 10th ed. International Centre for Prison Studies: London.

Walmsley, R. 2014. World pre-trial/remand imprisonment list, 2nd ed. International Centre for Prison Studies: London.

In: Imprisonment and Incarceration
Editor: Hillary N. Clarkson
ISBN: 978-1-63482-117-9

Chapter 3

EDUCATION IN THE CONTEXT OF DEPRIVATION OF LIBERTY: SENSES ATTRIBUTED TO WOMEN IN THE PROCESS OF SCHOOLING

Maria Celeste Reis Fernandes de Souza**[*,1]**,
Eunice Maria Nazarethe Nonato**[2]**,
***and Maria Gabriela Parenti Bicalho**[3]*
[1] Universidade Federal de Sergipe, Brasil
[2] Universidade Vale do Rio Doce, Brasil
[3] Universidade Federal de Juiz de Fora, Brasil

ABSTRACT

This paper forms part of the discussion on education in prisons, which has received attention in the field of human rights. The right to education in the context of deprivation of liberty is on the agenda of international discussions, and is aligned to the concerns about the situation of women prisoners. The empirical material was collected in a research that analyzed the constitution of all school educational experiences of women, young and adults, in situations of imprisonment in 04 Brazilian exclusively female prisons. The discussions presented in the article refer specifically to reports produced on interviews with 11 women

[*] celeste.br@gmail.com.

who attend school in one of these institutions. The analysis of the narratives produced by the interviewees takes as reference the theory of the relationship with knowledge proposed by Bernard Charlot, in a specific manner, the concepts of mobilization, direction and activity. The reports of the school experiences show two different situations regarding the conditions of access and permanence in basic education: trajectories marked by difficulties, stopped early, others more regular and long lasting. The prison is therefore for some women, the possibility of resuming the elementary school, for others, the inability to pursue high school. Despite these differences, it is possible to identify the aspects common to the reports, regarding the senses of school education, the mobilization in relation to learning and the positive effects of schooling. These aspects are presented and discussed as elements of understanding the complex reality of the education of women in the prison system.

Keywords: relationship to knowledge; gender; prison system; education for youth and adults – EJA

Study Context

This article seeks to contribute to the discussion on the education of women in situations of deprivation of liberty. According to data released by the Ministry of Justice (BRAZIL, 2008), it is possible to realize, in recent years, an increasing trend of women in this situation. According to the National Rapporteur on the Human Right, on the document "Educação nas Prisões Brasileiras: "almost 80% of women do not have the complete primary education" (CARREIRA, 2009, p. 28).

In the last decade, we have followed in Brazil, concerns about the recognition of the right to Education in trapping situation, by civil society, organized movements for human rights, educators, the judicial system, governments, researchers, culminating in 2010 with the approval and publication of the National Curriculum Guidelines for Prison Education (BRAZIL, 2010).

The educational opportunities offered to women in the prison units of the country have been discussed and, in many aspects, questioned, by the extension of the offer, or by the effectiveness of this offer in the continuity of women's studies (GRACIANO, 2005; GRACIANO and SCHILLING, 2008; NONATO, 2010 and 2011; YAMAMOTO *et al.* 2010; SOUZA, CAETANO and ROSA, 2012).

The purpose of this article is to broaden discussions on the supply of education in institutions of deprivation of liberty and gender correlations. Data were collected in a research that analyzed the constitution of schooling educational experiences of women in trapping position in the State of Minas Gerais[1]. The investigated field covers exclusively 04 female prison institutions of this state and in this text we deepen the analysis of interviews performed with 11 women who study in two of the surveyed prisons. The choice of the interviewees included different age groups and different educational backgrounds, without attempting to generate a representative sample.

Analyzing school trajectories of women, we take gender as a category of analysis (SCOTT, 1990). Therefore, studies that lead us to understand gender as produced in and producing social relations (LOURO, 1997) and as "social construction of gender difference" (PERROT, 2005, p.467) as guidelines of the way we look at analysis of the interviews.

We found in the theory of relationship with knowledge of Bernard Charlot (1999, 2000, 2001, 2005) an approach through which we could dialogue with the gender studies in the data analysis. From this point of view, it is not possible to think the knowledge neither the subject of knowledge out of the subject's relationship to knowledge, that is, knowledge can only be thought as a relationship. This relationship is established by a subject in a world that is prior to it, built in the relations of other subjects. Considering the perspective of the "sociology of the subject" proposed by Charlot (2000), the analysis considered both the social determinants of educational backgrounds experienced by women (in their early trajectory and also in the school prison institution) as the fundamentally subjective nature of these trajectories and experiences. We point out, in the interpretation of research data, three elements that Charlot (2000) presents as constituting the "relationship to knowledge": direction, mobilization and activity.

TRAJECTORIES AND SCHOOL EXPERIENCES

[1]Survey conducted with the support of the Conselho Nacional de Desenvolvimento Científico e Tecnológico – CNPq/Brasil.

There were eleven women who provided stories of their educational experiences: Lia, Sam, Ema, Sun, Sue, Mia, Ann, Eva, Pam, Kim, Peg. The analysis of the school experiences reports shows two different situations regarding the conditions of access and permanence in basic education: trajectories marked by difficulties and interrupted early and others more regular and permanent. The prison is for some women, the possibility of resuming the elementary school, and for others, the impossibility of continuing the high school. Despite these differences, it is possible to identify common aspects in the reports, with regard to the senses of school education, the mobilization in relation to learning and performing activities in the prison school. Referring these two situations we divided the reports of the interviews into two groups.

In the first group, we find Lia, Sun, Pam, Sue, Mia, Ann, Eva. They had their school trajectory interrupted by economic difficulties, discrimination, by early pregnancy. It is revealed in these trajectories the absence of the right of access and continuity of school life. For them, paradoxically, the prison was the opportunity to resume their studies, opportunity they estimate that they would not have in liberty. They reveal the concern and dedication to the orientation of sons and daughters in order not to drop out of school, showing how the concerns with the care mark the lives of these women.

Sue, 34, reports that stopped studying at 14 and returned at 16. She explains the reason for the interruption: "*I stopped because I got pregnant. Then I came back with 16, did the 5th grade, then stopped studying. I started working, then I stopped studying.*"

She had two daughters, one at 14 and another at 16. The relationship between pregnancy in youth and the difficulty in pursuing studies appear in the lives of Sue and her two daughters, who became pregnant at the age of 14 for the first time, and had three children. Thus, Sue was a mother at the age of 14, grandmother at 28 and by the time she was 34, she had six grandchildren. The oldest daughter, Sam now 22, was arrested along with her. The younger daughter also stopped studying, *"now there's no one to watch the kids, because I and Sam're arrested."*.

Sue relates school trajectory marked by repetition, *"I repeated the 3rd grade three times"*. She states that *"did not like to study, I just went"*. This "feature" she also identifies in her daughter Sam, who, like her, also *"did not have much interest"* in the studies. Mother and daughter returned to study in prison. Sue had been arrested about three years prior to the interview, initially in an institution that did not offer schooling opportunity. The previous year she had been transferred and soon resumed her studies, *"Then I came here and last year I did the 5th and the 6th and this year I'm doing the 7th and the 8th."*

Sam, on the other hand, who was serving her sentence at the same institution that her mother had completed the eighth grade and did not have provided, in deprivation of liberty condition, access to further study at the high school level. Sue comments positively about the possibility of studying, speaking of herself and her daughter, but regrets the lack of high school offer, reflecting that if the provision in the prison institution is not possible, there should be the opportunity to study in schools outside the institution. In their condition of deprivation of liberty, Sue speaks of the studies as a need for integration in the labor market, and calculates the time it would take to complete high school, if she could study the following year: "*And I doing the first year, let's assume that I will make the 1st year in six months, things end up in the middle of the year I'm leaving. When I get there on the street I get the same study design that has here of six months?*

She also shows concern for the certification of schooling made in the prison institution, *"Let me tell you, this diploma we take here serves to get service there on the street normally?"*. She states that she wants to do high school to *"get a better job, change of life,"* since *"what is important is the degree, not matter what. (...). Because today the person who has no education, poor thing, is like me."*

For Sue the condition of deprivation of liberty provided an opportunity to advance in the achievement of elementary school, and she worries about the continuity of studies, in and out of prison. The recognition of the importance of schooling reflects the awareness of the imposition of formal schooling requirement, for someone who had an exclusion from school trajectory.

Lia, 30, had studied up to the fourth grade of elementary school. She began her schooling at the age of 7, and stopped at the fifth grade: *"I started school I was seven, I did the 1st, 2nd, 3rd, 4th. So I started the 5th and left school, I stopped studying, I started working."* She tried to return to school at night, but did not go on: *"I began to see that could not study the night because it was way too dangerous neighborhood, I stopped studying."* The situation of deprivation of liberty brought opportunity to resume her studies, *"... Only thank God here I returned to school, I want to go back to school when I get out of here"* According to her, dropping out of school in the fifth grade happened against the will of her mother: *"I was supposed to renew my registration, and I said: - Mother I will not study more. Then my mom [said]: - no, my daughter studies."* Now, back to school, in prison, she lives a situation similar to her own daughter, *"and my daughter is now 14 years old and did not want to go to school. Then I sent a letter to her talking about the same as my mother said."* When asked if she would be studying if not arrested, she said she did not think so, *"because I did not have any incentive. Get it? I would be just like this: no, I will not study! I had already stopped!"*

The opportunity to return to school in prison also appears in what is concerned to the regulation of school documentation. Lia, who had no records of her passage in school, is exposed to an evaluation process performed by the educator and is included in adult education class and can enroll in a school after leaving prison, a desire she manifests in the interview.

Pam, 40, had studied up to the fifth grade of elementary school. She reports a childhood with many hardships and problems, including the mother's alcoholism, which prevented her of monitoring and stimulating the school life of Pam and her three sisters. When talking about the reasons that led to leaving school, there were two aspects: the discrimination suffered for being black and the need to help her mother raise her younger sisters. She reports: *"I did not have much affection from my mother. To continue my studies. And it was a lot of suffering in my childhood, so I had suffered humiliation at school. I dropped out of school, I went to work, I left the school."*.

In an attempt to provide the sons and daughters a different situation, sought to stimulate their schooling, which she relates including with the crime committed.

> This whole prison was to be able to keep them study, something that I did not have opportunity I gave them to study, something that my mother never was able to give me I gave to them, to study, they were always very well dressed to school, very neat to not even have to suffer what I suffered. And then it was where they studied. I even encouraged them to go to school. My boy left school, dropped, but I am leaving now I'll see if I talk to him, he's seventeen.

In prison, she resumed her studies. *"I just made up the fifth grade, I only did the fifth, now I'm doing the fifth and the sixth, next year I'm going to the seventh, God willing I will finish."*

Kat, 53, before being arrested, had attended school until the second year of elementary school. She talks about the beginning of her school life in the countryside, the long walk she had to take, with her brothers, to get to a very poor school. She studied at the countryside until the second year, and then stopped studying. She moved to the city at the age of 10, her mother enrolled her in school again, but she *"did not want to study."* She got married early and had three daughters. She separated from her husband, and to support her daughters, she went to work. She went back to school in prison.[2]

Mia, 51, recounts her life in school: "*I only have grade 1, only the 1st year of school, I know nothing. I cannot read. That letter there, I do not know, I do not know anything, I know the letters, but I do not know put words, sentences*". She does, however, know many things: "*Now math I know almost all. I can work all, I do work of manual embroidery, I do everything I can do anything, but I cannot read. God gives me a lot of wisdom, have no education, but my father raised me*".

Mia tells of her schooling experiences in childhood and in other prisons in which she fulfilled part of her sentence. Of the school she attended as a child, she reports the difficulties: "*I lived on the farm and it was too far, lots of ox...I am 51 years old, parentes before would not let girls out. And then we ran from the ox, ran and did not learn anything, just got beated, the teacher beated a lot and I did not learn anything*".

She concludes that, in her family, *"almost no one learned to read, learned after adult."*. She had also studied in other prisons, but said she did not learn much because *"We leave the prison with bad head"* About the school in prison, she says: *"I´m getting better now. I´m learning. Now I can do something."* For her, it is important to learn to read and write *"to take care of my children, my grandchildren. I want to leave here and go back to another life "*, and to *"not rely on others"* [in prison institution, to write or read the letters through which she communicates with family members].

Eva, 34 years. The narrative of her trajectory brings the deprivation of the right to education for poor girls, explicitly. She says she entered the school at 9 years old, because of her mother's initiative, and had *"...a willingness to learn, to be something. My dream was to be a teacher at the time."* But after the holidays, her mother took her out of school, because only her brothers on her father (Eva was the daughter from a previous relationship) would have condition to study, *"because they had father (...). And I was her daughter, but the daughter of another man, I am the oldest of the house, but when she married another man she already had me. Then I was not studying, I started working in the countryside."*

At 12 Eva left home to work as a maid, at 14 moved in with a guy she met, whom she broke up some time later. With another companion, she had three daughters. She concludes: *"Then my youth passed. Without that*

---

[2]The name of the interviewees is fictitious.

opportunity of study, a person to give me that opportunity: What I wanted to be in life."

Therefore, her poor family condition led Eva to a life story in which work, relationships and motherhood took the place of studies. These could have allowed, in her view, to choose "what she wanted to be in life." She sees herself, therefore, as someone who lived without being able to choose. In prison institution, Eva went back to school. Reports what she learned: *"So a few I read, I learned to write my name. I read, but to write I do not write, because I can even write, but misses some letters "*. She says she has. *"... Very desire, will to learn, especially when people sit near me and have the patience."* She believes that the fact that she is learning will give her a new perspective on her relationships with others: *"... when I leave here I can show out there, show them, even my relatives, in return, the difference, as I had the ability to learn."*

Being able to learn means to her a difference to the way people will see her, among those people she highlights her daughters: *"To be something to show for my daughters. Get there in front also I'm sure my daughters, I'm sure my kids will be interested too."* Eva wants her daughters to enjoy what she did not *".My dream is see my daughters better studied and formed."*

Ann, 58, says: "*I never studied because could not afford, my parents never had conditions, I struggled with great difficulty, to help my brothers, so I never had the opportunity to study, but I had long wanted to study because the person who do not read, like me, fight hard".*

She reports that it was important to study in prison, says she made an identity document, highlighting her joy to be able to sign her name, without suffering the *"humiliation of having to put my finger"*: *"I am studying, I am learning something... now I've written my name on the identity and made all my documents and thank God I did homework this week and I am learning."*

The interview with Ann reveals two different ways to talk about herself, initially presented as someone who did not study and cannot read. Throughout the interview, while she tells that she learned to read in school prison institution, she talks about what she can do, and also what she could already do, even without reading.

Lia, Sun, Pam, Sue, Mia, Ann and Eva have in common the school trajectory marked by difficulties and interrupted early. They found in prison the possibility of going back to school, and talk about the importance of this study, to themselves and for the care of family members. Two other interviewees produced reports presenting situations different from the previous. Sam, Ema, Kim and Peg advanced much more in education, with paths marked by school success, despite the difficulties faced. Therefore, they do not find the possibility of continuing studies in the situation of deprivation of liberty. They have to demand the completion of high school and higher education.

Ema, 24, was arrested in her second year of high school, in Normal course of a traditional school of the city. She reports a regular trajectory, school success, which was interrupted by prison. While studying, she dreamed of studying Administration. At the time of the interview, she wanted the opportunity to attend the second and third year of high school while serving her sentence, because there was still a year to finish fulfill it. *"So I'm trying to do two years in one, I want to study at the school near here"*. Asked if she would have that opportunity, she says that *"if we chase, we can. Talking to the judge that comes here once a month, he gives the opportunity..."*

Sam, 22, began studying at 7 years old and stopped at 14, in eighth grade, because she became pregnant and had *"no condition to go to school. I had no one to leave my son and I had to take a mother responsibility, but my dream was to go back to school. My dream is still to finish study and go to college."* She returned to study in the prison institution to complete the eighth grade, seven years after leaving school. However, although important, the offer of studies in the prison unit will not be enough for Sam to continue studying after the end of primary education, since there is no offer of secondary education.

Ema and Sam demonstrate the construction of a positive view of themselves as students, claim that they had facility in the subjects, good grades, and they liked the school. Ema even not benefiting from the certification offered by the school, attended classes, to remember what she had learned. The two were in an institution that offered schooling only up to the level of the final years of elementary school, and did not enjoy the right to study at a school outside the prison institution.

Two other young girls have similar profile, but were in an institution that had the opportunity to attend high school. Kim, 23, said she had always been a good student, and highlights the role of her mother that *"wanted us to study, do college ..."* She followed a regular school trajectory without reproofs, but dropped out of school *"On third year, I started to get involved with people, and it took me from the school"* What happened next was narrated by the young girl *"then I stopped studying, I left home, I was lost, so I was arrested."*

Kim was initially taken to another prison institution, in which, she said, *"there was no opportunity to study."* When she arrived at the institution in which she was, she was not studying for two years, discovered that she could study, and completed the third year of high school. She highlighted the participation in the graduation in which the presence of the family was permitted, *"Two people from each family and then our mother deliver us a degree, it's all very cool. And it was good not only the matter of study which we need too."*

She says she plans to attend college of Physiotherapy or Administration, and she took the National Examination for Secondary Education (ENEM) in the prison institution. She speaks of the other women who study at the institution, noting that she likes to follow those that begin in the early years of elementary school, some arriving unable to read or write.

Peg, 28, reports the interruption of a successful school trajectory, which culminated in the arrest:

> I always liked studying and got good grades, but when I got involved with drugs, I left the studies. The director of my school called my mother because I was skipping school and since I had good grades, she called my mother and talked to her. Uh ...why is Peg not coming in class? We want her to come back, for her to conclude, this was the last year of high. Then my mother came and talked to me, but I was already using a lot of drugs and I could not go back to school.

Despite the efforts of her mother and the school principal, Peg says that the course she had taken in her life did not allow her to think about going back to school, *"I'll be quite honest, when I was on the street I did not imagine myself studying more. The life I was leading, companies, all made me think of not studying"*. The difficulties experienced after the arrest led her to realize the necessity to study:

> We need to learn, especially in the legal area (...) so I can leave. Then I started to get interested to do craft. Then I had to study, so I took the course of criminal law. Then I started to study in the cell to find a way out of here, it was when I started studying. For me to do a craft I needed to have a good Portuguese, good grammar, then I started taking grammar book.

She says she studied her penalty survey and found an error, and she wrote the letter asking for a correction. The return to the classroom was not, however, experienced by Peg without difficulties. Away from school for ten years, she imagined that she was not going to succeed anymore: *"I thought, I'll get lost inside the classroom, I will not be able to do anything, I will not understand anything, I will not remember. I just think, what we learn, what we truly learn we do not forget"*.

After completing high school, Peg has no option to continuity of schooling. She says she misses participating in educational experiences developed in the prison institution, *"I miss a lot, sometimes I talk to Luciene (school principal): Luciene let me get back to study!? I can do the third year again ... "* Unable to attend school, Peg continues to study alone, to attempt ENEM. She speaks of a redemption of the will to study: "*On the street I did not imagine myself studying more. So I had to come to prison to rescue in me the will to study. Now I want to study again. Because I want to do a course in fashion design".*

While unable to fulfill this desire, Peg takes other courses offered in the prison institution, such as computer and administrative assistant: *"I loved it, I was a star student in the course. And I never dreamed of doing a course of administrative assistant."* The return to school and the courses were important for the redemption of her relationships with her family. Peg says that her father abandoned her when she entered the "world of crime". With the return to school, however, the father recontacted his daughter. "*Today he follows my trajectory here. One day I called him then he said: my daughter I'm very happy with you; do not think I'm not watching you .I know you did that course and that you graduated from high school".*

Peg takes education as a family value, and speaks of what she intends to do to ensure that her younger brother continue to study. "*And today my fight will be with my brother and I know the importance today, went through this all and he will have to study. (...). I'll take him to class every day, I insist on taking and picking him up".*

The recognition of the differences between the school trajectories of women prisoners is important and places for education different issues and demands. To deal with these issues, we resume the theory of relationship to knowledge proposed by Charlot (2000, 2005), which proposes the understanding of the subject as at the same time, and in all, a human being, a social being and a singular being. A desire being in a world shared with other subjects; who occupies a social position with the family as the first instance and attributes senses and singular meanings to himself and the world, in building an unique story. For this subject, learning is a necessity that marks its presence in a knowledge-producing world. This activity is central to the human construction process, which involves becoming a member of the human species, an unique human being and a member of a community, occupying it. Through education produces itself and is produced by the world. Therefore, the subject and its story are always fully social and totally singular, and membership in a social class is interpreted in an active manner by individuals in the construction of a story in which they are the subject. In dialogue with the Sociology of Pierre Bourdieu, the author states that it is necessary to analyze the activities that individuals exercise in the context of social positions, to "... win, to maintain, to 'pass' these positions and we also need to consider other persepctivas than simply their social position "(CHARLOT, 2005, p.40).

For the obligation of learning how to be, which, according to the author, underlies the human condition, subjects experience different processes of learning, in which different relationships with different knowledge are established, different relationships with learning in different contexts.

> The relationship with knowledge is the set of relations that an individual establishes with an object, a 'thought content', an activity, an interpersonal relationship, a place, a person, a situation, an occasion, an obligation, etc. related in some way to learn and to knowledge - therefore, it is also related to the language, relationship with time, with activity in the world and over the world, relationships with others and relationship with themselves, as more or less able to learn such a thing in such a situation (CHARLOT, 2005, p.45).

The relationship with knowledge is, therefore, constituted by a set of relationships undertaken with diverse ways of learning that vary according to the situation posed by the type of knowledge and the circumstances in which learning occurs. This notion is opposed to "negative" analysis, the one that identifies the elements that "are missing" to the subject to achieve the proper attitude towards learning. Thus, it is erroneous to be concerned about finding "the" relationship with knowledge of the subject, ignoring the different spaces, situations and interactions involved in the educational process in which this subject participates. "The research on the relationship with knowledge must then analyze the different elements that integrate the processes built by the subject in the various interactions" (CHARLOT, 2001, p.15-16).

About the data analyzed, we ask: what components are part of the processes built by women students of schools in prisons in the interactions they experience in school? Such elements are, on one hand, in their school trajectories: to what extent they could enjoy the right to education? In what ways the other demands - maternity, work, love relationships, relationship with the world of crime, access conditions - interfered in their "decision" to leave school? What did they learn? How do they see themselves as learners (more or less able to learn)?

In the brief presentation we made of the women interviewed in this section, the elements of the school trajectory are outlined, showing the diversity of school courses and the image they built of themselves. Then, in our conclusions, we continue with the presentation of the theoretical framework of relationship with knowledge proposed by Bernard Charlot to discuss the meanings of schooling for these women.

TO CONCLUDE: MEANINGS OF SCHOOLING

The analysis of the relationship with knowledge leads the author to the concepts of mobilization, activity and meaning, "what is analyzed here as relationship works as a process that develops itself in time and involves activities" (CHARLOT, 2000, p 54.). In order to have activity, the subject must be mobilized and for this, the situation must present meaning.

The concept of mobilization refers to the internal dynamic needed to learn. To mobilize is to put in motion. "To mobilize means to put resources in motion. To mobilize is gather strength, to make use of oneself as a resource "(CHARLOT, 2000, p.55). The definition of mobilization involves the concept of activity, the author states that the subject

> ... mobilizes oneself, in an activity, when you invest in it, when you use yourself as a resource, when it is set in motion by mobiles that refer to a desire, a meaning, a value. The activity has, then, an internal dynamic. One should not forget, however, that this dynamic implies an exchange with the world, where we can find desirable goals, action means and other resources than itself (CHARLOT, 2000, p.55).

According to the author, the adoption of the term activity intends to emphasize the presence of a subject who performs it. Subject that mobilizes, puts themselves in motion according to certain activities. To understand this dynamic, Charlot still uses the concept of meaning.

This concept is explained by the author by a triple definition: the possibility of establishing relations in a system or set, the possibility of establishing relations with other aspects or facts of life of the subject and the production of intelligibility about something. Thus, it makes sense "what is communicable and can be understood in an exchange with others. In summary, the meaning is produced by establishing relationship, within a system, or in relations with the world or with others "(CHARLOT, 2000, p.57). These three concepts have been adopted in the reading we did of the reports produced by women in the interviews.

We can begin this reflection by asking: When attending schools of prisons, in relation to what and in what ways the interviewed mobilize? How to make "use of self" in these processes? In the reports produced by them, we find the mobilization in relation to "a normal life"(the movement is toward the outside, what they can enjoy when they are in freedom if they have advanced in their schooling) and also in relation to learning in school, learning content, learning typically scholastic skills (in this case, the movement is centripetal, that is, they move towards the own school knowledge). Let's look at the two situations:

> "I'm close to leaving, now I'm going back to study and intend to follow my normal life! A life of a normal human being" (Lia).
>
> "It is very good to study. Today I see that is important, because if you want a job you have to get to the 3rd, so the study is needed. Today I can see what is really important" (Pam).
>
> "I think I changed, because now I think further ahead. I study more, grow more to give a good life for my son" (Ema).

These data show a mobilization regarding the future, for which education is a secure track, or an external requirement. The following data show that there is also the mobilization in relation to school knowledge. Lia, for example, shows great satisfaction in learning, and it stands out even when responding to a question about the redemption of the penalty for days studied: "*Of course I wanted my redemption, would help me a lot in my process. And again I wanted to learn what I did not know, many things I did not know that today I already know. For example, to interpret text. I never imagined that I could interpret a text*".

Ema has already completed the elementary school and attended some classes, *"just to pick up some things, much time that I did not study. I wanted. For when I were in the semi-open I go to school already remembering some things I forgot. "*.

Commenting on other school students is when Ema reveals her enchantment in relation to learning: "*There are many girls here that did not know to read and write, they learned a lot here. There are people here who could not read and now put the letters together already. They do not speak to us, they speak so quietly, softly, I'm paying attention to: - Oh, learned! Then they are laughing for nothing (laughs). I like to see when they are joining the alphabet too, is cute*".

Sam, when asked what she likes at school, says, "experience". When explaining her response, talks about the involvement with the "new stories" of each day: *"I find it very interesting because every day, especially in mathematics... mainly history and geography, every day is a new story. Then you get involved in that, I find it very good."*

Besides the mobilization, we can read the reports produced in the interviews from the perspective of the concept of meaning. Recalling the definition of Charlot presented above, we ask: what makes sense in school education experienced in prison? Despite the mobilization in relation to learning, the interviewees did not report to school content as elements that "make sense", help to understand the world, have relation to something they did or knew before. What seems to bring different ways of understanding life, or living, is the relationship with teachers, more specifically, the fact that school teachers treat them well, are interested in their lives and see them as capable of learning. Some examples:

When asked about what she enjoyed most in school, Lia refers to the content, and then emphasize the relationship with the teacher, *"I like everything. My problem is more math, but the teacher is wonderful. Mariza, I do not know if you know .. She explains and explains again and I'm getting. Teachers who give classes here are wonderful, super treat people well, for them we are not even prisoners".*

In the case of Lia, the satisfaction with the learning of the interpretation of texts begins with the recognition that she could interpret texts, which begins with the intervention of the teacher, an attitude of appreciation of the student: *"And Sueli (teacher) said so: - Lia you are great at reading comprehension. I went, ah, Sueli, stops ... And she's teaching me the paragraphs where I can put point where I cannot. "*

The dialogue below, starting from the question of the interviewer, also shows how the interest of the teachers is what seems to make sense in school:

Interviewer: - and what is it like in the class?

Lia: - ah the teacher arrives, says good afternoon, asks if everything is ok ... And if we have any news of our process we talk to them, they listen.

Interviewer: - What kind of news?

Lia: - Like on the 16 I have a forum [audience]. So I arrive like that: Oh, teacher! I heard right? So I get to the teacher: - on the 16 I have a forum! So they are happy in the same way that we get! They are good people!

Similar aspects are present in the story of Ema:

> I faced a whole new world of all I'd forgotten, but little by little I was remembering. And it's very good! Teachers that come without any fear of coming, though knowing that're messing with arrested people, it is not easy but they come with an open heart, willing to help, offer a friend shoulder, to be more than a teacher, it is important for us.

In Sun's interview, the link established with the teacher relies on an aspect often criticized regarding the EJA: the infantilization. In recounting her trajectory, she says she stopped studying on the "infancy" and the conversation continues as follows:

Interviewer: *But then after that you never studied, only when you came here?*

Sun: *only when I came here. They evaluated me and gave me a test. Sueli (teacher of Portuguese and English Language) is an amazing person.*

Interviewer: *Is it true*

Sun: *So she treated me as if I were a child. Then more students came and I even started to feel jealous, said: it is okay now you despise me! I joked too much, she's really nice. I really like her.*

Peg has built her renewed interest in studies from the attention received from a teacher who complimented her letter. "*The teacher encouraged me, Gislaine. She said: wow your letter is beautiful! And I was very capricious with my notebook, she was encouraging me and for me it was a moment that I was helped the most here*".

Finally, we might ask ourselves about the activities developed by women in school. In interviews, they do not discuss activities they perform, emphasizing, as we have seen, qualities and attitudes of teachers. Other times of the data collection process provides feedback that can help understand this "absence". The visits to the institution and the conversations we had with the women in situation of deprivation of liberty made us see that the possibilities of educational activities involving discussion of topics, argumentation and research do not find space in the school, because it has no place in the prison institution.

In addition, interpersonal relationships in schools of prison institutions follow their own standards of prison institution, involving surveillance and suspicion among women themselves. This complicates the implementation of activities that escape a vertical learning relationship, which would involve dialogue and exchange of knowledge.

The EJA recognizes the importance of the life of the subjects being present in educational practices. At school in prisons seems to be no room for life: on the one hand, the earlier life can not be invoked, as would bring the reality of the infringement and losses related to it. On the other hand, imposes itself the silencing of anxieties, needs, and the grievances the present life.

REFERENCES

Brasil (2008). *Sistema Penitenciário no Brasil:* dados consolidados. Brasília, 2008. Available: www.portal.mj.gov.br/data/pages . Access: 25/09/ 2012.

Brasil (2010). Resolução CNE/CEB 2/2010. *Diário Oficial da União,* Brasília, 20 de maio de 2010, Seção 1, p. 20.

Carrreira, D. (2009). *Relatoria Nacional para o Direito Humano à Educação:* Educação nas Prisões Brasileiras. São Paulo: Plataforma DhESCA. Brasil. Available: http://www.dhescbrasil.org.br Access: 06/04/ 2012.

Charlot, B. (2000). *Relação com o saber. Elementos para uma teoria.* Porto Alegre: Artes Médicas Sul.

Charlot, B. (2001). *Os jovens e o saber:* perspectivas mundiais. Porto Alegre: Artmed Editora.

Charlot. B. (2005). *Relação com o saber:* Formação dos professores e globalização. Questões para a educação hoje. Porto Alegre: Artmed,.

Graciano, M. (2005). *A educação como direito humano:* a escola na prisão. 165f. Dissertação (Mestrado em Educação) - Faculdade de Educação, Universidade de São Paulo, São Paulo.

Graciano, M.; Schilling, F.(2008). A educação na prisão: hesitações, limites e possibilidades. *Estudos de Sociologia,* Araraquara, v.13, n.25, p.111-132.

Louro, G. L. (1997). *Gênero, Sexualidade e Educação:* Uma perspectiva pós-estruturalista. Petrópolis: Vozes.

Nonato, E. M. N.(2010). *Educação de mulheres em situação prisional:* experiência que vem do sul, no processo de reinvenção social. 198f. Tese (Doutorado em Ciências Sociais). Universidade do Vale do Rio dos Sinos, Porto Alegre.

Nonato, E. M. N. Educação de mulheres em situação de privação de liberdade. In: Ireland, T. D. (Org.)(2011). Educação em prisões. Brasília: INEP; Brasília: *Em Aberto*, v. 24, n. 86, p. 127-140.

Perrot, M. (2005). *As mulheres e os silêncios da História.* Bauru, SP: EDUSP.

Scott, J. (1990) Gênero: uma categoria útil de análise histórica. *Educação e Realidade.* Porto Alegre,v.20, n.2, p.5-22, jul/dez.

Souza, M. C. R. F.; Caetano, C. S.; Rosa, S. F. (2012).Educação de mulheres em situação de aprisionamento: reflexões sobre o perfil social e o direito à educação. Available:http://35reuniao.anped.org.br/images /stories/posteres /GT18/GT18- 1501_int.pdf.

Yamamoto, A. *et al.Cereja Discute: educação em prisões.* São Paulo: Alfa Sol: Cereja, 2010.

In: Imprisonment and Incarceration
Editor: Hillary N. Clarkson

ISBN: 978-1-63482-117-9

Chapter 4

Desistance from Heroin Use and Ex-prisoner's Life Narratives of Reform in Hong Kong

***Wing Hong Chui**[*,1]* ***and Ryan Holmes**[2]*

[1] Department of Applied Social Sciences; City University of Hong Kong, Kowloon, Hong Kong

[2] School of Social Science; The University of Queensland; Queensland, Australia

Abstract

This study presents an in-depth investigation of reform through interpreting how a selected group of men who have desisted from heroin-use understand and present their change process. It consisted of ten life narratives including the stories of seven successful desisters and three active offenders living in Hong Kong. The 'opportunity' sample was recruited with the assistance of one non-governmental organization which provides help with discharged prisoners. Based upon the interview data, a thematic content analysis revealed that successful desistance was dependent upon two contingencies, namely deterioration of physical health and religious conviction. In addition, an actor's display of agency through readiness and openness to change was the precursor for establishing an identity shift incompatible with continued criminal

[*]E-mail address: eric.chui@cityu.edu.hk.

behavior. Belief in the good core self encouraged ex-prisoners to achieve 'earned redemption' through engaging in generative pursuits. Desistance from drug-use behavior can be explained with reference to the interplay between individual decision and life-changes.

Keywords: desistance, heroin, ex-prisoners, narratives, agency, structure, Hong Kong

INTRODUCTION

Desistance from crime refers to the cessation of offending and is encapsulated as a process by which individuals often assume the role of a non-offender or 'reformed person' (McNeill, 2004; Farrall and Calverley, 2006; Abrams, 2012; Opsal, 2012; King, 2013; Bakken, DeCamp and Visher, 2014; Healy, 2014). Reflected by the visible dearth of research compared with studies examining onset, persistence, and escalation of criminal offending, however, criminologists to date have just begun to devote more attention to deriving a theoretical understanding of the latter stage of the criminal career model – the desistance process. In fact, although most offenders eventually stop committing crimes, the various circumstances under which offenders may be encouraged to relinquish their criminal lifestyle and the maintaining mechanisms underlying the desistance process represent complementing versions of social phenomena not fully understood within the realm of criminology. In this respect, knowledge about the processes of desistance is clearly critical to identifying how and why ex-offenders come to change their behaviors (Farrall and Bowling, 1999; McNeill, 2004; Massoglia and Uggen, 2010; Murray, 2012; Forrest, 2014; Harris, 2014; Liem and Richardson, 2014; Wyse, Harding and Morenoff, 2014).

This chapter examines the process of drug desistance by examining the life-narratives of ten males living in Hong Kong. It is divided into five sections. The second section presents an overview of the correctional system for drug offenders. The third section reviews the current literature on desistance. In the fourth section, information regarding the sample is provided and the qualitative methods used to analyze the data are discussed. In the fifth and final section, results are organized according to the perceived subjective changes in the definitions of oneself and significant events in one's life that emerged from the interviews when exploring the elemental ideas of: the core self, sense of agency, and generative motivations.

CUSTODY FOR DRUG OFFENDERS IN HONG KONG

The Correctional Services Department is solely responsible for enforcing the court orders for prisoners. There are different types of prison or custody, namely the maximum security prison, the medium security prison, the minimum security prison, the training center, the rehabilitation center, the detention center and the half-way house (Chui and Lo, 2008; Correctional Services Department, 2014a). Since it is beyond the scope of this paper to look at all of these institutions, the following discussion will primarily focus on the context of a minimum security prison which exclusively accommodates male adult drug offenders, that is the Drug Addiction Treatment Center (DATC). Vagg (1994) opined that while the way the authorities manage all prison establishments is the same, the DATC places more emphasis on detoxification, and elimination of psychological and emotional dependence than others. According to section 4(1) of *Drug Addiction Treatment Centers Ordinance* (Cap. 244), 'where a person is found guilty of a relevant offence and the court is satisfied that in the circumstances of the case and having regard to his character and previous conduct it is in his interest and the public interest that he should undergo a period of cure and rehabilitation in an addiction treatment center, the court may, in lieu of imposing any other sentence, order that such person be detained in an addiction treatment center'. The length of detention is usually not less than 2 months and not more than a year according to the ordinance. As indicated in section 5(1) of the Ordinance, those discharged prisoners from DATC are supervised by the aftercare or rehabilitation officers of the CSD. Breaching the conditions of the supervision order or aftercare supervision is a criminal offence, and the person concerned is liable to a fine of HK$5,000 and imprisonment for a year. As set out in section 6(1) of the Ordinance, if the discharged prisoner fails to comply with the requirements of the supervision order, it is also possible for the Commissioner to '... make a recall order against such person requiring him to return to an addiction treatment center; and thereupon such person may be arrested and taken to an addiction treatment center and detained there'.

The rehabilitation model of criminal justice policy and practice is still valid in Hong Kong, and 'giving an offender a second chance to reform and to be rehabilitated' has been emphasized in both community-based and custodial sentences (Adorjan and Chui, 2012, 2013; Chui, 1999, 2001, 2003; Chui and Gelsthorpe, 2004; Chui and Lo, 2008; Chui and Cheng, 2013). The stated mission of the CSD (2014b) is to 'detain persons committed to [the] custody in a decent and healthy environment, and provide comprehensive rehabilitative services in a secure, safe, humane and cost effective manner, so as to enhance the physical and psychological health of prisoners, protect the public and help reduce crime'. Since January 1998, a new division titled Rehabilitation Division has been set up, and this division consists of five units, including a pre-sentence assessment panel, aftercare unit, education unit, vocational training unit, and psychological services section. The ultimate goal of drug rehabilitation in the correctional setting is to help reduce re-offending behavior. Admittedly, the extent to which this form of correctional rehabilitation has achieved its stated goals has remained unknown and is yet to be subject to systematic investigation. This chapter aims to fill the gap by analyzing the process of desistance among ten ex-prisoners who served their time in the DATC or other institutions in Hong Kong.

A Review of Drug Desistance Literature

In general terms, desistance refers to a cessation of offending activity among those who have offended in the past. Most criminologists define desistance as the state of having 'terminated' offending. As a result, empirical measures of desistance emphasize the state of non-offending rather than the process of desistance (Bushway *et al.*, 2001). Essentially, this focus on the final state of non-offending ignores the nature of the process by which individuals reach their final state of non-offending (Buscema, 1998). It also disregards the fact that 'criminal behavior is sporadic with "termination" taking place all of the time' (Maruna, 2001, p. 23). Recently, however, criminologists have begun to re-examine and expand the definition of desistance to include attention to the process by which people arrive at this state of non-offending (Bushway *et al.*, 2001). Uggen and Kruttschnitt (1998), for example, use the term 'behavioral desistance', suggesting that desistance has two implicit components: a change from offending to non-offending and the arrival at a permanent state of non-offending. Based on such reasoning, it is recognized as imperative within this area of research to distinguish termination of offending from the concept of desistance. Specifically, 'termination is the time at which criminal activity stops. Desistance, by contrast, is the causal process that supports the termination of offending' (Laub and Sampson, 2001, p. 11). Consequently, the operationalization of desistance employed within this paper places an emphasis on gradual processes. Such a measure effectively distinguishes desistance as the 'process of reduction in the frequency and severity of [crime], leading to its eventual end when "true desistance" or "quitting" occurs' (Fagan, 1989, p. 380).

Maruna (2001) identifies three broad theoretical perspectives in the desistance literature: maturational reform, social bonds theory and narrative theory. Maturational reform theories are based on established links between age and criminal behavior. From this, 'ageing is the only factor which emerges as significant in the reformative process' (Glueck and Glueck, 1940, p. 105). Associated with the idea of physiological 'burn out', the basic idea of this approach is that desistance is the result of offenders growing out of crime and settling down. Reflected by Gottfredson and Hirschi's (1990) adaptation of the Gluecks' approach, 'maturational reform continues, almost by default, to be one of the most influential theories of desistance in criminology' (Maruna, 1999, p. 297).

Social bonds theories suggest that ties to family, employment and education create a stake in conformity (a reason to go, and stay, straight) and explain changes in criminal behavior due to the potential loss when continuing to offend. For instance, Sampson and Laub (1993) argue that changes in crime are due to variations in informal social control or social bonds that are independent of age. As a result, the authors strongly maintain that decreases in offending are not due to the 'inexorable aging of the organism' (Gottfredson and Hirschi, 1990, p. 141), but result from the strengthening of the social bond through investment in 'institutional forces associated with employment, marriage, prison, [and] parenthood ... that often accompanies movement into adult roles and responsibilities' (Ezell and Cohen, 2005, p. 34).

Narrative theories have emerged from more qualitative research and value the significance of subjective changes in the person's sense of self and identity, as reflected in changing motivations, greater concern for others and more consideration of the future. By and large, self-narratives explain individuals' actions in a sequence of events that connect up to explanatory goals, motivations and feelings, thereby shaping and guiding future behavior. What this provides is a 'logical, believable, and respectable story' about who the individual is that 'makes it impossible to engage in criminal conduct without arousing guilt reactions and feelings of shame that are incompatible with the self-conception' (Cressey, 1963, p. 158; cited in Maruna, 2001, p. 86). To date, however, only a few empirical studies have addressed the concept of narrative identity and desistance from crime and delinquency. In retrospective interviews with ex-offenders, Irwin (1970), Mulvey and LaRosa (1986), Graham and Bowling (1995) and Shover (1996) have all found indications that a change in identity and self-concept is critical to the process of reform (see also Gadd and Farrall, 2004).

Evidently, desistance resides somewhere in the interfaces between developing personal maturity, changing social bonds associated with certain life transitions, and the individual subjective narrative constructions which offenders build around these key events and changes (McNeill, 2003). It is not just the events and changes that matter; it is what these events and changes mean to the people involved. Accordingly, turning points and structural supports may be necessary conditions for desistance but they are not sufficient. Individual action needs to align with the social structure to produce (and maintain) behavioral change, and 'theories of the life course have been remiss to have left agency – which is essentially human social action – largely out of the theoretical picture' (Sampson and Laub, 2005, p. 177). Considering this, while not denying the importance of ageing and structural factors, conscious effort is made herein to reposition human agency as a central element in understanding crime and desistance over the life-course.

Maruna (2001) provides an important focus on subjective orientations in the desistance process by repositioning the individual as a central element within the theoretical landscape. This major contribution to desistance theory and narrative methodology alike introduces three key themes characterizing how desistance works, namely generative motivations, the core self, and sense of agency.

Combining these themes with the four intimately related cognitive transformation types (openness to change; exposure/reaction; conventional replacement self; definition transformation) proposed by Giordano *et al.* (2002), this paper endeavors to broadly investigate these themes (also referred to as "hooks for change") through empirical research into these elements in the Hong Kong context. Essentially, this intends to emphasize the actor's role in creatively and selectively appropriating agents in the environment which prompt shifts in identity and changes in the meaning and desirability of drug-use behavior.

As such, the criminological desire to capture the 'up front' work accomplished by actors as they make initial moves toward a different way of life and determining whether these elements will serve well as catalysts for lasting change pose the research question: What subjective changes in definitions of oneself and significant events in one's life influence the successful accomplishment (and sustained maintenance) of a disengagement from drug-using criminal careers?

METHOD

Stimulated by the infancy of the narrative method within the desistance literature, this study considers how subjective changes in definitions of oneself and significant events in one's life influence the successful accomplishment (and sustained maintenance) of a disengagement from drug-using criminal careers. Collected narratives are empirically analyzed to provide explanations of *how* this sample have individually rebuilt, remodelled or remade, and subsequently maintained, their own social identities. The self-narrative is increasingly understood as a critical part of an individual's personality and inner self (see McAdams, 1985; Giddens, 1991) to guide and organize human behavior patterns, thereby providing life with a sense of meaning (Singer, 1997). Interest in these narratives, however, is not so much concerned with the facts they contain (what happened) but rather in the meanings an individual attaches to such facts. Therefore, although the narratives collected in this research are largely retrospective accounts of past events, this is not a retrospective study that looks at people who have 'already desisted' and asks them how they did it or what made them change. Rather, this is a study investigating and documenting people actively 'making good' (Maruna, 2001) with a dominant emphasis on maintenance processes.

During the three weeks of fieldwork, three participants declined to be interviewed for several reasons such as "having no time" and "refusal to go through the painful experience". In this study, ten male participants were recruited with the assistance of one non-governmental organization which provides help to discharged prisoners in Hong Kong. They had completed all supervision orders associated with their prison sentence for at least three years. They are still affiliated with this non-governmental organization for various reasons such as seeking help with employment as well as financial support, and participating in social and volunteer activities. When asking about their repeated drug misuse or re-offending behavior, seven claimed that they were 'clean'; and three admitted taking drugs occasionally with these behaviors going unnoticed. Table 1 shows the demographic profile of the participant.

Participants range in age from 37 to 62 years, and the majority of participants are over their fifties. Two self-identify themselves as Christian, one as a Buddhist and the remaining seven have no religion. Three of them have children and their marital status varies between married, divorced/separated or single within the sample. Unemployment is the most consistent theme across all individual cases and only one respondent holds full time employment. Not included within the table for aesthetical purposes, heroin was/is the drug of choice for the desisters/persisters and unemployment strongly associates with increased dependence on government benefits.

Table 1. Demographic Profile of the Participant

Age	Lapses or relapses to drugs (Yes/No)	Religion	Marital Status	Employment
37	No	No	Married with 3 children	Working (Part-time)
38	Yes	Buddhist	Single	Unemployed
52	No	Buddhist	Married	Unemployed
53	Yes	No	Single	Unemployed
54	No	Christian	Separated	Unemployed
54	Yes	No	Divorced	Unemployed
55	No	Christian	Single	Unemployed
58	No	No	Married	Working (Part-time)
59	No	Christian	Divorced with 1 child	Unemployed
62	No	No	Married with 1 child	Working (Full-time)

Individual semi-structured interviews were conducted with ten participants, and each interview lasted approximately 90 minutes. After collecting demographic data (age, marital and parental status, educational level attained, employment status, and religiosity) and verifying each participant's official and self-reported involvement in crime, interviews investigated key themes emerging from the literature. Allowing considerable scope and flexibility, the main focus of the interviews was to encourage participants to 'tell their story'. Participants were asked open-ended, topical questions concerning perceptions of family, law enforcement and criminal justice, education and employment experiences, chronologies of relationships with significant people, illicit drug use, participation in selling drugs, substance abuse intervention programs, gang affiliation, significant life events, and the context and process of crime cessation. Consistently addressing these topics within every interview effectively ensured each participant adequately covered significant life stages and agents contributing to their socialization, regardless of their past experiences and current self-identified position within society.

Each taped interview was initially transcribed verbatim in Chinese, followed by translation into English. Data were then subjected to a qualitative content analysis approach, which is informed in part by the phenomenology perspective. It emphasizes the subjective nature of the social world as well as the meaning of social actions (Chan, 1997). Thematic content analysis involves 'coding' or 'scoring' verbal material for manifest (rather than latent) content to assess the cognitive characteristics of a sample of individuals (Smith, 1992). This process of 'thought sampling' (Murray, 1943; cited in Maruna, 2001) preserves the richness and meaning of each participant's life narrative while rendering the data comparable across individual cases.

RESULTS

All participants confirmed the well-established addictive significance of heroin use and the subsequent discomfort when withdrawing the substance from a dependent system. One commented:

> I was addicted for 30 years … I made a mess for my past. I never wanted to be like that. In the past I knew some bad friends but I thought I wouldn't become a drug addict. However, when I was a teenager, my friend bought a bag [of heroin] and shared it with a few of us. I had a good feeling after tasting it and got addicted after taking it a few times. I felt uncomfortable and got cold if I hadn't taken it. (Desister, 59)

Prison was overwhelmingly criticized for its failure to act as a catalyst for lasting change. Rather considered as a "holiday", prison allowed offenders to "learn more bad things and know more bad people" (Persister, 38). In effect, desisters failed to exclusively attribute their conforming transformation as a product of "time served" due to the lack of prospective intervention in the form of education and skill development. For example, one said:

> It is not useful to be held in prison. They just tell us not to re-offend without teaching us what we should do after discharging from the prison. What "rehabilitative service" do they provide for us? They never teach us what we should do and how we should analyze something right or wrong after discharging from prison. They just keep saying, "You will be arrested if you keep taking drugs". [Desister, 58]

A General Cognitive Openness to Change

While it was recognized by participants that drug treatment programs in prison were of no use in dealing with their drug misuse, the interview data indicated that one core element for their drug desistance was the motivation to take action to change one's life for the better. Explained by one participant: "unless heroin addicts are decisive to quit taking drugs, they can't quit it, no matter who they are" (Persister, 38). Consequently, an initial openness or overall "readiness" to change consistently appeared to be a minimal starting point in the move toward a more conforming way of life:

> Several times I nearly died … I took too much heroin and was sent to hospital. I stayed in [Intensive Care Unit] for a few days. I was in bed like that four times … I hoped I could have a new life. [Desister, 37]

Beyond the superficial attractiveness of "turning over a new leaf", however, it was revealed that lasting changes frequently needed to be built upon processes that are ultimately more tangible than desire and good intentions. Specifically, chances for successful change were greatly enhanced when the individual engaged in experiences that have good conventionalizing potential. Several informants made at least some reference of their exposure to God, with some narratives almost completely dominated by positively internalized religious references:

> Let me explain by using a sentence by an English writer. He said: "Plato represents the wisdom in Seattle whereas Confucius represents wisdom in Asia". But the writer, Peter, thinks that you could desist from crimes if you trust Christ. That means religion gave me the motive to desist from crimes. I wanted to take drugs again when I quit it at the beginning … So I have to fight against the drugs. I believe the Christ, so the Father, the Son and the Holy Spirit would help me to fight against the temptations of the drugs. [Desister, 55]

Consistent with religion, children served as an important focus around which to initiate behavioral changes as well. Nevertheless, considering the long-distance relationships maintained by some individuals to conceal their drug-addiction, exposure to the presence of children failed to reliably constitute a powerful impetus for desistance since the accompanying attitudinal elements were missing. When present, however, the following statement illustrates the receptivity of the change agent due to personal recognition of internal adjustments:

> I stopped taking drugs completely when my son entered the University of Hong Kong. He knew I was a drug addict and I could feel that he disliked me taking drugs … I felt ashamed. He did not encourage me to quit, I quit [drugs] because I felt ashamed. [Desister, 58]

From this, it appears the increasing allure of conventionality derives from the conflict between a strong deviant identity and its associated behaviors and the demands of alternative prosocial identities which acquire new value (in this case, parent). Logically, marital partners also proved influential catalysts within the actors' social network for changes in life direction:

> I nearly got divorced with my wife. At that time I was completely helpless … totally depressed. I felt that the sacrifice was too big. I should not get divorced with my wife because of heroin. So I can conclude that my turning point is my wife. I don't want to give her up. [Desister, 52]

For those men not married, however, "external certification" from some outside positive source similarly provided this conforming motivation which was enmeshed in unfamiliar feelings of being cared for and respected. Specifically, reported empowerment in the form "no one has ever taken this sort of chance on me" permitted individuals to develop an attitude of self-value which personally restored (or established) their faith in the moral goodness of society:

> The Chaplain at St Stephen Church was so good to me. He always came to see me and talked to me regularly. He cared for my situation. Although he could not give me any financial support, when I didn't have money for lunch he would get me some, when I didn't have clothes he would buy me some. At that time I was really touched to see others were so good to me. At the beginning, I quitted heroin because I would like to reward them. [Desister, 54]

Identity Shift – Envisioning an Appealing and Conventional "Replacement Self"

Consistent with unprecedented and unanticipated redemption, shocking experiences and the subsequent "moment of clarity" they provided were also connected with successful disengagement from drug use. While a few participants mentioned that acquaintances and old school classmates had lost legs because of taking drugs by injection, a rather dramatic cognitive transformation was linked to a disturbing or shocking experience. Essentially, this enabled the actor to craft a satisfying replacement self that was seen as incompatible with continued criminal behavior:

> My close friend and I went to the sixth floor of a building at Yau Ma Tei to inject heroin … the amount I injected was less than him. I injected half dose per time and he injected one pill per time. After he injected it, he couldn't stand it. The person in charge said he was not okay and asked me to take him away. I tried to wake him up, such as hitting his face … Then I called 999 for emergency. After two days, he died … There are many impurities in today's heroin … you cannot predict the consequence. That's why I am afraid of taking heroin. [Desister, 37]

Maintaining Change through Generative Intention

Effectively confirming the initial openness to change as a fundamental prerequisite in the move toward a more conforming way of life, the narratives further highlighted the agentic factor of personal motivation in maintaining "what you want to become". This was conveyed through consideration of the "many consequences to be human beings" and produced a shift in identity which involved a transformation in the way the actor viewed drug-use behavior and the lifestyle itself:

> I haven't considered drugs again because I know there must be some consequence if I take drugs again. It is bad to do so even when I have money to buy drugs because it would affect my wife, my daughter and my health. [Desister, 62]

Actively upholding these "responsibilities" transpired into individuals engaging in generative pursuits. This enabled actors to envision and begin to fashion an appealing and conventional "replacement self" that could supplement the marginal one associated with heroin use. Expressing a desire for "something to show" by "giving back to society", desisters described rewarding pleasures in other-centered activities through special attachments to a particular group or cause:

> The Chaplain arranged a course for me which is widening my social circle ... The church wants to help me. But they are not only choosing me. They are also choosing many people. I have to follow "my brothers and sisters" who have similar backgrounds with me. This helps me a lot because although they are sometimes weak, I learn how I was in the past from them. When I help them, I help myself. [Desister, 54]

Generative intention and the want "to be good for myself" was often prompted by the acknowledgement of past "destruction" along with the realization that time and life is a diminishing resource: "... I regret for what I did in the past. That feeling is very hard. I regret that I lost my life by taking drugs" [Desister, 55].

Self-Doubt within the "Good Core Self"

Concessions of remorse and recognition of the immorality of past behavior saw the internalization of shame as a necessary prerequisite for belief in the "good core self". This positive self-mastery allowed the narrator to "move on" via dominant control over his destiny: "I got a job, quit heroin and gained my dignity. I now have a normal life" [Desister, 37]. However, one desister contended that such "control" simply accounts for the here and now due to the prospective uncertainty that may inhibit everlasting success:

> Frankly speaking, I may take drugs again after 10 years, or I may commit suicide in the future. None can predict the future. But I am sure that I am decisive to quit drugs now. [Desister, 55]

Recognition of "self-scepticism" inevitably suggested a "limit" whereby individual control could not proceed, but simply be maintained. Considered optimistic due to pure "hope" navigating the intent to remain legitimate, this highlights the possibility that desisters, not active offenders, are the true 'reality distorters'. In fact, although admitting the wrongfulness and potentially dangerous consequences of heroin abuse, persisters conveyed a strong sense of control through a confident display of self-realism and fulfilment:

> If I really listened to what my father said I could have quit my addiction in the past. But I just want to pursue the "free" enjoyment in my life right now. Do you understand? [Persister, 54]

Despite actions speaking louder than words, the latter excerpt suggests success is obtainable, but not internally valued. Self-assurance that heroin fills one's life with content reads while irregular, active offenders are explicit in what they want and unconditionally fulfil such desires.

> Many people in Hong Kong are worse than me. I am not the only one who takes drugs, there are many. Some people will lie down on the floor once they take drugs and others won't care. [Persister, 54]

Therefore being rendered incapable of declaring socially respected success, active offenders reported feelings of victory in alternative aspects of daily life. For example, while admittedly being unable to quit the addiction, achievements such as "getting out more" were triumphantly interpreted, disregarding the unintended consequence of increasing negative peer association. This mindset emerged from addictive behavior generating (and reinforcing) addictive thinking, which enabled internalization of the self-concept normal-user in control. Importantly, this differentiates from the addicted user out of control:

> I saw another drug addict a few days ago. His leg is rotted. I told him that he has to consult a doctor immediately, otherwise two consequences will result. One, he will die when the bacteria goes to the brain. The other, he will lose his leg after a month. Finally, he consulted a doctor and is now being treated in hospital. [Persister, 54]

Discussion and Conclusion

Results derived from the narratives effectively confirm that desistance is a process which may be induced, reaffirmed or disturbed by events, but is inadequately theorized as a singular moment. Moreover, the process is likely to be gradual because it is emotionally and physically painful, not necessarily unidirectional, and highly contingent upon the capacity of significant others. From this, the data reinforces the idea that researchers would be wise to differentiate 'primary desistance' – a kind of 'crime-free gap' in the life-course – from 'secondary desistance'. The latter is best described as 'the movement from the behavior of non-offending to the assumption of a role or identity of non-offender' (Maruna and Farrall, 2004, p. 174).

Consistent with both Maruna (2001) and Farrall (2002), the narratives of the participants demonstrate that successful desistance (including its maintenance) depends upon social and psychological contingencies. These interpersonal and temporal contingencies include: the fundamental desire for change; mental and physical health; religious affiliation;[1] a shift in identity; the evolution of relationships with partners, parents and children; the ability to reconstruct one's past as part of a 'generative script' with a shift from self-absorption to concern for others; and finally, the belief of significant others, sometimes culminating in feelings of reintegration or 'earned redemption'. Overall, the events and experiences associated with desistance have exerted their effect by bringing about changes in these ex-offenders' self identity and sense of responsibility. This strongly supports the process of desistance as one which is 'produced through an interplay between *individual choices*, and a range of wider social forces, institutional and societal practices ... beyond the control of the individual' (Farrall and Bowling, 1999, p. 261, emphasis added).

For example, many desisters in this study attributed positive change to the "want to be good to the self". At the same time, however, desisters spoke of their "necessary reform" as a result of internalized shame and the perceived negative image drug-use casts on significant others, particularly their immediate family. Consider the father who abstained from heroin to create a positive image and provide a supportive role for his son entering university. Also present within this theme were 'newfound contacts' who had 'taken a chance' on these individuals and orchestrated conventional routine which the ex-offender valued. Take the example of the 54 year old desister who was so overwhelmed by the constant and generous support he received from the Chaplain – who himself was not financially equipped to help others – that he quit heroin as a sign of respect and gratefulness.

Similarly, the discovery (and acceptance) of religion provoked a shift in conforming identity: "The main reason for me to quit from drug addiction is because of religion. I believe in Christ and I understand the philosophy of the Bible" [Desister, 55]. Commonly, this theme led to the development of a generative script whereby ex-offenders redeemed their destructive pasts by giving something back to society. These 'other-centered' pursuits advanced the future generation, took responsibility for the existing older generation, and enabled the activation of wounded healer attributes to reform those with similar backgrounds to the ex-offender. Significantly, this shift from self-

[1]What must be recognized is the paradox in some spirituality-based conversion narratives whereby one gains personal control by explicitly "giving up" personal control to the will of a higher spirit. This research asserts the apparent contradiction (giving up control in order to be free) should still be seen as agentic in nature since the person freely chooses to give over his life to God (Maruna, 2001).

absorption to concern for others largely connected with epiphanies of shocking experiences and the radical reconsideration of desired mental and physical health.

Clearly, the environment can thus provide a kind of scaffolding that makes possible the construction of significant life changes. Nonetheless, individuals themselves must attend to these new possibilities, discard old habits, and begin the process of crafting a different way of life. While many have referred to potentially prosocial features of the environment as catalysts, change agents, or even turning points (Laub and Sampson, 2001; Maruna, 2001), the results confirm the logic of calling them "hooks for change" (Giordano *et al.*, 2002). Primarily, this is because actors' accounts within a narrative or life history will not access the full array of influences that produced successful changes. Instead, narratives have hooks – 'shorthand ways to describe what seems essential from the communicator's point of view' (Giordano *et al.*, 2002, p. 1000).

Undeniably, cognitive transformations are an important component of significant and sustained behavior change from a drug taking career. As the measured variable 'hope' demonstrates, an actor's overall readiness or openness to change represents the first, and arguably the most fundamental ingredient necessary for an individual to realign with mainstream values. However, for a person to desist, ambition by itself is insufficient since one's attitude is an equally important element in successful change. Drawing attention to the change catalysts that feature heavily in the desistance stories, there appears to exist individual variation in receptivity to particular agents, as well as variations in the transformative potential of the agents themselves (refer to the presence of children). Consequently, an important consideration is the degree to which a catalyst enables the actor to craft a satisfying replacement self (for example, good husband, positive role model or hard worker) that is seen as incompatible with continued criminal behavior.

On the flipside, the results also demonstrate how addictive behavior generates addictive thinking which typically results in a self-concept of normal-user in control (see Gorski and Miller, 1991). Consequently, the storied identity of the persistent offender seems to be based upon a great number of glaring contradictions and discrepancies. Belief in the good core self among active offenders emerged as the chief example. For instance, within Maruna's (2001) sample, the long-term, persistent offenders talked at length about wanting to go clean but feeling powerless to achieve this using their own volition. Findings within this study, however, indicate that committed active offenders possess a high level of social control. While undeniably unconventional, this control nevertheless saw offenders unconditionally enjoying fulfilled lives by only pursuing "obtainable circumstance". Therefore opposing Maruna's 'distortion view', the findings here propose it is rather the persisting active-offenders whose narratives seem the most out of step with reality since they fail to consider all human possibility, regardless of the difficulty.

In this study, the absence within the narratives of ageing accounting for behavioral change casts significant doubt over the explanatory power of maturational theory as an independently reliable answer to the desistance process. In opposition to the body of literature prompted by Glueck and Glueck (1940), ageing did not emerge as significant in the reformative process and was not associated with the idea of physiological 'burn out'. While some desisters did make small acknowledgements of growing older, the adverse health effects associated with continued drug abuse were cited as more influential in the consideration to abstain from heroin than old age per se. Persisters noted age-appropriate activities they should be engaging in (for example, having tea in a restaurant), though these were bluntly overridden and dismissed via confessions that desistance is a difficult process. Consequently, due to the deeply addictive nature of opiate addiction and the 'free' sensation it provides for those who use it, it is considered that feelings of tiredness or 'burn out' may be alleviated through heroin continuation. This is not to suggest maturational theory fails to account for other categories of crime (for instance, property crime), but in cases of serious drug addiction with the associated symptoms of withdrawal, perhaps an opposing effect occurs whereby so-called exhaustion from ageing maintains the behavior due to the strenuous commitment required to remove the substance from the dependent system. This seems conceivable when taking into account the views of one persister who suggests his old age prevents any solution to help quit his addiction. Specifically, with the increase of age, taking drugs became a more attractive option for persisters due to the perception that youth is required for the worthwhile struggle for one's life.

Also, in this study, not a single participant indicated the experience of prison giving rise to thoughts of change – failing to support 'the pains of imprisonment' put forward by Baskin and Sommers (1998). While some considered the consequences of life on the streets following discharge and the negative image of returning to prison on those close to them, such thoughts do not match the experience of prison as 'an imposing accumulation of aggravations and deprivations' like Shover (1983, p. 217) reported. Instead, change followed obtainment of 'something' the desister valued or relocation into a new geographical niche.[2] This positions control theory (Hirschi, 1969) as a useful theoretical perspective for the provision of after-care services since what seems to matter in prisoners' resettlement is the social environment to which they return: the support of family and friends; and a situation which fosters law-abiding behavior and attitudes. To accommodate these findings, improvements within rehabilitative initiatives are paramount. General developments could include promoting access to establishing religion or spirituality (Bakken, DeCamp and Visher, 2014), expanding conventional social networks through enhancing decision making strategies (Campbell and Hansen, 2012), and enlarging the mechanisms to allow and maintain intense and profound family contact (Wooditch, Tang and Taxman, 2014), especially amongst drug using offenders. The consistent theme here maintains that interventions should not be focused solely on the individual person and their perceived deficits. As Farrall (2002) notes, the problem with such interventions is that while they can build human capital, for example, in terms of enhanced cognitive skills or improved employability, they cannot generate the social capital that resides in the relationships through which we achieve participation and inclusion in society (Adorjan and Chui, 2014; Chui and Cheng, 2014). Rather, since desistance has related more clearly to people's motivations and to the social and personal contexts in which various obstacles to desistance were addressed, it appears that developing strengths-based (rather than needs-based) approaches is a plausible response (McNeill, 2006; Saleebey, 2012).

REFERENCES

Adorjan, M. and W.H. Chui (2012) 'Making Sense of Going Straight: Personal Accounts of Male Ex-prisoners in Hong Kong', *British Journal of Criminology*, 52(3), 577-590.

Adorjan, M. and W.H. Chui (2014) 'Aging Out of Crime: Resettlement Challenges Facing Male Ex-prisoners in Hong Kong', *The Prison Journal*, 94(1), 97-117.

[2]Some men reported rather dramatic relocations (for example, rural Mainland China) which raises interest (not suspicion) in the contradiction of distancing oneself from structural supports (for example, family and community support centers) that were simultaneously found as important factors for change. Future research should closely examine how such "moves" can be maintained in the absence of familiar support.

Abrams, L.S. (2012) 'Envisioning Life "On the Outs": Exit Narratives of Incarcerated Male Youth', *International Journal of Offender Therapy and Comparative Criminology*, 56(6), 877-896.

Bakken, N.W., DeCamp, W. and C.A. Visher (2014) 'Spirituality and Desistance from Substance Use among Reentering Offenders', *International Journal of Offender Therapy and Comparative Criminology*, 58(11), 1321-1339.

Baskin, D.R. and I.B. Sommers (1998) *Casualties of Community Disorder: Women's Careers in Violent Crime*. Boulder, CO: Westview.

Buscema, M. (1988) 'A Brief Overview and Introduction to Artificial Neural Networks', *Substance Use & Misuse*, 37(8-10), 1093-1148.

Bushway, S., A. Piquero, L. Boidy, E. Cauffman and P. Mazerolle (2001) 'An Empirical Framework for Studying Desistance as a Process', *Criminology*, 39(2), 496-515.

Campbell, H. and T. Hansen (2012) 'Getting Out of Game: Desistance from Drug Trafficking', *International Journal of Drug Policy*, 23(6), 481-487.

Chan, J. (1997) 'Understanding Juvenile Crime: A Review of Traditional and Contemporary Theories', in A. Borowski and I. O'Connor (eds) *Juvenile Crime, Justice and Corrections* (pp. 25-42). Melbourne: Addison Wesley Longman.

Chui, W.H. (1999) 'Residential Treatment Programs for Young Offenders in Hong Kong: A Report', *International Journal of Offender Therapy and Comparative Criminology*, 43(3), 308-321.

Chui, W.H. (2001) 'Theoretical Underpinnings of Community-based Sentences and Custody for Young Offenders in Hong Kong', *Hong Kong Law Journal*, 31(2), 266-282.

Chui, W.H. (2003) 'Experiences of Probation Supervision in Hong Kong: Listening to the Young Adult Offenders', *Journal of Criminal Justice*, 31(6), 567-577.

Chui, W.H. and K.K.Y. Cheng (2013) 'The Mark of an Ex-prisoner: Perceived Discrimination and Self-stigma of Young Men after Prison in Hong Kong', *Deviant Behavior*, 34(8), 671-684.

Chui, W.H. and K.K.Y. Cheng (2014) 'Challenges Facing Young Men Returning from Incarceration in Hong Kong', *Howard Journal of Criminal Justice*, 53(4), 411-427.

Chui, W.H. and L. Gelsthorpe (2004) 'In the Eyes of Hong Kong Chinese Female Drug Offenders', *Australian and New Zealand Journal of Criminology*, 37(Supplement), 107-121.

Chui, W.H. and T.W. Lo (Eds.) (2008) *Understanding Criminal Justice in Hong Kong*. London: Routlegde.

Davis, C., Bahr, S.J. and C. Ward (2013). 'The Process of Offender Reintegration: Perceptions of What Helps Prisoners Reenter Society', *Criminology & Criminal Justice*, 13(4), 446-469.

Correctional Services Department (2014a) *Types of Facilities*. Hong Kong: Correctional Services Department. Available at: http://www.csd.gov.hk /english/facility/facility_type/ins_ins.html

Correctional Services Department (2014b) *Vision, Mission and Values*. Hong Kong: Correctional Services Department. Available at: http://www.csd.gov.hk/english/about/about_vmv/abt_vis.html

Cressey, D.E. (1963) 'Social Psychological Theory for Using Deviants to Control Deviation', in *Experiment in Cultural Expansion: Proceedings of the Conference on "The Use of Products of a Social Problem in Coping with the Problem Norco, CA*" (pp. 147-160). Washington DC: National Institute of Mental Health.

Ezell, M.E. and L.E. Cohen (2005) *Desisting from Crime: Continuity and Change in Long Term Crime Patterns of Serious Chronic Offenders*. Oxford: Oxford University Press.

Fagan, J. (1989) 'Cessation of Family Violence: Deterrence and Dissuasion', in L. Ohlin and M. Torny (eds) *Crime and Justice: An Annual Review of Research*, Vol. 11 (pp. 357-426). Chicago: Chicago University Press.

Farrall, S. (2002) *Rethinking What Works with Offenders: Probation, Social Context and Desistance from Crime*. Cullompton: Willan.

Farrall, S. and B. Bowling (1999) 'Structuration, Human Development and Desistance from Crime', *British Journal of Criminology*, 39(2), 252-267.

Farrall, S. and A. Calverley (2006) *Understanding Desistance from Crime: Theoretical Directions in Resettlement and Rehabilitation*. Maidenhead: Open University Press.

Forrest, W. (2014) 'Cohabitation, Relationship Quality, and Desistance from Crime', *Journal of Marriage and Family*, 76(3), 539-556.

Gadd, D. and S. Farrall (2004) 'Criminal Careers, Desistance and Subjectivity: Interpreting Men's Narratives of Change', *Theoretical Criminology*, 8(2), 123-55.

Giddens, A. (1991) *Modernity and Self-Identity: Self and Society in the Late Modern Age*. Stanford, CA: Stanford University Press.

Giordano, P.C., S.A. Cernkovich and J.L. Rudolph (2002) 'Gender, Crime and Desistance: Toward a Theory of Cognitive Transformation', *American Journal of Sociology*, 107(4): 990-1064.

Glueck, S. and E. Glueck (1940) *Juvenile Delinquents Grow Up*. New York: Commonwealth Fund.

Gorski, T.T. and M. Miller (1991) *Understanding Addictive Disease: A Tool for Preventing Relapse*. Independence: Herald House.

Gottfredson, M.R. and T. Hirschi (1990) *A General Theory of Crime*. California: Stanford University Press.

Graham, J. and B. Bowling (1995) *Young People and Crime*. London: Home Office.

Harris, D.A. (2014) 'Desistance from Sexual Offending: Findings from 21 Life History Narratives', *Journal of Interpersonal Violence*, 29(9), 1554-1578.

Healy, D. (2013) 'Changing Fate? Agency and the Desistance Process', *Theoretical Criminology*, 17(4), 557-574.

Hirschi, T. (1969) *Causes of Delinquency*. Berkeley: University of Chicago Press.

King, S. (2013) 'Transformative Agency and Desistance from Crime', *Criminology & Criminal Justice*, 13(3), 317-335.

Irwin, J. (1970) *The Felon*. Englewood Cliffs, NJ: Prentice Hall.

Laub, J.H. and R.J. Sampson (2001) 'Understanding Desistance from Crime', in M.H. Tonry and N. Norris (eds) *Crime and Justice: An Annual Review of Research*, Vol. 26 (pp. 1-78). Chicago: University of Chicago Press.

Leverentz, A. (2010) 'People, Places, and Things: How Female Ex-prisoners Negotiate their Neighborhood Context', *Journal of Contemporary Ethnography*, 39(6), 646-681.

Liem, M. and Richardson, N.J. (2014) 'The Role of Transformation Narratives in Desistance among Released Lifers', *Criminal Justice and Behavior*, 41(6), 692-712.

Maruna, S. (1999) 'Criminology, Desistance and the Psychology of the Stranger', in D. Canter and L. Alison (eds) *The Social Psychology of Crime: Groups, Teams and Networks* (pp. 287-320). Aldershot: Ashgate.

Maruna, S. (2001) *Making Good: How Ex-convicts Reform and Rebuild their Lives*. Washington, DC: American Psychological Association.

Maruna, S. and S. Farrall (2004) 'Desistance from Crime: A Theoretical Reformulation', *Kolner Zeitschrift fur Soziologie und Sozialpsychologie*, 43, 171-194.

Massoglia, M. and Uggen, C. (2010) 'Settling Down and Aging Out: Toward an Interactionist Theory of Desistance and the Transition to Adulthood', *American Journal of Sociology*, 116(2), 543-582.

McAdams, D.P. (1985) *Power, Intimacy and the Life Story: Personological Inquiries into Identity*. New York: Guilford Press.

McNeill, F. (2003) 'Desistance-focused Probation Practice', in W.H. Chui and M. Nellis (eds) *Moving Probation Forward: Evidence, Arguments and Practice* (pp. 146-162). Harlow: Pearson Education.

McNeill, F. (2004) 'Desistance, Rehabilitation and Correctionalism: Developments and Prospects in Scotland', *Howard Journal of Criminal Justice*, 43(4): 420-36.

McNeill, F. (2006) 'A Desistance Paradigm for Offender Management', *Criminology & Criminal Justice*, 6(1), 39-62.

Mulvey, E.P. and J.F. LaRosa (1986) 'Delinquency Cessation and Adolescent Development: Preliminary Data', *American Journal of Orthopsychiatry*, 56(2), 212-24.

Murray, C.A. (2012) 'Young People's Perspectives: The Trials and Tribulations of Going Straight', *Criminology & Criminal Justice*, 12(1), 25-40.

Murray, H.A. (1943) *Thematic Apperception Test Manual*. Cambridge, MA: Harvard University Press.

Opsal, T. (2012) ''Livin' on the Straights': Identity, Desistance, and Work among Women Post-incarceration', *Sociological Inquiry*, 82(3), 378-403.

Saleebey, D. (Ed.) (2012) *The Strengths Perspective in Social Work Practice* (6th ed.). Boston, MA: Allym & Bacon.

Sampson, R.J. and J.H. Laub (1993) *Crime in the Making: Pathways and Turning Points Through Life*. Cambridge, MA: Harvard University Press.

Sampson, R.J. and J.H. Laub (2005) 'A General Age-Graded Theory of Crime: Lessons Learned and the Future of Life-Course Criminology', in D.P. Farrington (ed) *Advances in Criminological Theory: Integrated Developmental and Life-Course Theories of Offending*, Vol. 14 (pp. 165-81). New Brunswick, NJ: Transaction Publishers.

Shover, N. (1983) 'The Latter Stages of Ordinary Property Offender Careers', *Social Problems*, 31(2), 208-18.

Shover, N. (1996) *Great Pretenders: Pursuits and Careers of Persistent Thieves*. Boulder, CO: Westview.

Singer, J.A. (1997) *Message in a Bottle: Stories of Men and Addiction*. New York: Free Press.

Smith, C.P. (1992) 'Inferences form Verbal Material', in C.P. Smith (ed) *Motivation and Personality: Handbook of Theoretic Content Analysis* (pp. 383-392). Cambridge: Cambridge University Press.

Uggen, C. and K. Kruttschnitt (1998) 'Crime in the Breaking: Gender Differences in Desistance', *Law and Society Review*, 32(2), 339-66.

Vagg, J. (1994) 'The Correctional Services Department', in M. Gaylord and H. Traver (eds) *Introduction to the Hong Kong Criminal Justice System* (pp. 145-160), Hong Kong: Hong Kong University Press.

Wooditch, A., Tang, L.L. and F.S. Taxman (2014) 'Which Criminogenic Need Changes Are Most Important in Promoting Desistance from Crime and Substance Use?', *Criminal Justice and Behavior*, 41(3), 276-299.

Wyse, J.J.B., Harding, D.J. and Morenoff, J.D. (2014) 'Romantic Relationships and Criminal Desistance: Pathways and Processes', *Sociological Forum*, 29(2), 365-385.

Legislation Cited

Drug Addiction Treatment Centers Ordinance (Cap. 244)

THE AUTHORS

Wing Hong Chui, Ph.D., Professor, Department of Applied Social Sciences, City University of Hong Kong. Prior to this, he was Associate Professor in the Department of Social Work and Social Administration at The University of Hong Kong. His areas of interest include youth studies, criminology, criminal justice, and social work. He is co-editor of several books, including *Moving Probation Forward* (with M. Nellis, 2003), *Social Work and Human Services Best Practice* (with J. Wilson, 2006), *Experiences of Transnational Chinese Migrants in the Asia-Pacific* (with D. Ip and R. Hibbins, 2006), *Research Methods for Law* (with M. McConville, 2007), and *Understanding Criminal Justice in Hong Kong* (with T.W. Lo, 2008).

Ryan Holmes, B.A. (First Class Honors), formerly part-time Research Assistant, School of Social Science, The University of Queensland, Australia.

INDEX

D

E

F

G

H

I

J

V

W

Y